ON MY WAY HOME
I BUMPED INTO GOD

But Not Really by Chance

RAYMOND J. GOLARZ
MARION J. GOLARZ

authorHOUSE®

AuthorHouse™
1663 Liberty Drive
Bloomington, IN 47403
www.authorhouse.com
Phone: 1 (800) 839-8640

Published by AuthorHouse 11/16/2016

ISBN: 978-1-5246-4918-0 (sc)
ISBN: 978-1-5246-4917-3 (e)

Library of Congress Control Number: 2016918654

Print information available on the last page.

Any people depicted in stock imagery provided by Thinkstock are models, and such images are being used for illustrative purposes only. Certain stock imagery © Thinkstock.

This book is printed on acid-free paper.

Because of the dynamic nature of the Internet, any web addresses or links contained in this book may have changed since publication and may no longer be valid. The views expressed in this work are solely those of the author and do not necessarily reflect the views of the publisher, and the publisher hereby disclaims any responsibility for them.

Scripture quotations are taken from the Douay-Rheims Version of the Holy Bible (DRV), American Edition published in 1899.

Table of Contents

Dedication

To Our Mothers

Helen Grelak Golarz

And

Marion O'Neil Simpson

Acknowledgments

We would first like to thank the following persons who were gracious enough to act as readers for the unpublished book. Their comments were invaluable to us. They gave us guidance that directed us to make some changes that we believe enhanced the readability and special message we were attempting to convey. These very special people are Father John Meany, O.P., Mrs. Anne Novak, Dr. Mary Smith and Mr. Tim Smith.

A special thank you goes to our son Thomas John Golarz for his assistance with computer skills that were beyond his parents' abilities.

Finally, to Dr. Bruce Smith, it is incredible how many essential editorial changes you recommended after we were sure we had a flawless document.

Preface

Until the softening currents of Vatican II wound their way into the religious instruction of Roman Catholic children, the essence of God was primarily distilled in the lessons contained in the Baltimore Catechism. The responsibility for passing on these articles of faith and knowledge fell primarily to the nuns who, until their ranks thinned in the latter part of the twentieth century, made up the teaching staffs of most parochial schools.

Very often religion was the first subject of the day. Beginning when they were as young as six, children lined up at the blackboard or stood in neat rows next to their desks to digest the first of their lessons which captured in sparse, straight-forward language, the most basic facts about God and the purpose for which He created us.

Over the years, the Baltimore Catechism underwent revisions. However, the lessons which spelled out the doctrine of the one true church were couched in essentially the same language. Thus, most children experienced their introduction to theology in the same manner. A typical session would progress in question-and-answer style.

Nun: "Jean, who made you?"

Jean: "God made me."

Nun: "Mary, why did God make you?"

Mary: "God made me to know Him, to love Him, and to serve Him."

Nun: "David, why else did God make you?"

David: "God made me to serve Him in this world and to be happy with Him forever in the next."

So began the teaching of a message that was intended to shape an understanding of God that would be sufficient to guide these children to God's heavenly home.

Of course, the Baltimore Catechism was not the only basis for instruction. As children and young people moved through their parochial education, the Bible was a companion text. These students were introduced through the Old Testament to the historical and moral foundations in place up to the time of Christ. The New Testament was more heavily emphasized as it contained the words, acts, and sacrifice of Christ which had become the foundation of Christianity and because it further defined the ways in which the faithful could know, love, and serve God.

Children, especially as they matured, were called to absorb and emulate the way of life that Christ embodied. It was all there—the way to honor not just the rule but the spirit of the Ten Commandments. In parables, sermons, and in acts of kindness and profound sacrifice, Christ demonstrated what we needed to do in order to know this loving God. We needed to pray, to share our wealth, to forgive. We needed to speak truth, comfort the lonely, the stranger, and the oppressed. We needed to offer hope and healing to lost and damaged souls. Over and over again, the lessons attempted to provide the insights necessary not only to know God, but to understand our relationship to Him and His purpose for our lives.

Yet for untold numbers of believers, the profound import of these lessons either faded away or was never truly grasped. What remained were the most basic, parroted concepts—the lists of do's and don'ts. Thus, how to know, love, and serve God became for some a religious game—a game the purpose of which was to avoid committing a sin so grave that it would result in their being excluded from the church. Sadly, the true message of Christ also became obscured by the insecure, harsh, and unpredictable nature of life, leaving too little time or energy to ponder how to know and rest in the gift of God's love.

This failure to consciously and consistently respond to the profound demands and rewards of loving has left most of us unable to explain or find what our souls long to experience. Instead of hearing and feeling God's essence as a still whispering that lives in our souls, our concept of God is often that of a distant figure hidden somewhere above the clouds while His only-begotten son Jesus is locked into a narrative that casts him mostly as a necessary and effective mediator between us and God. Jesus, then, who despite His partly human nature, is now approachable only if one comes to worship, beg for forgiveness, or seek miracles. So, we move along dominated by the needs, joys, and losses life always brings. These needs and events distract us—often for long periods of time—from a nagging sense that something in our souls is lacking—some piece of knowing that gives our lives meaning, purpose, direction, understanding, and peace: *Enter, God.*

On My Way Home, I Bumped into God, is made up of stories and commentaries that explore how God acts directly and indirectly in our lives. Despite the common belief that we control most of our lives through our choices and our will, the message of this book suggests rather that God is constantly nudging us to follow a better path, that God does not leave us alone, and that He persists in attempting to get our attention by forever "bumping" into us.

You will find this belief conveyed through stories that recognize the integrity and worth of a homeless man on a street corner, the personal honor of a worker in a steel mill, the empathy of a brave brother, the strength of a grateful father, and the wisdom of peasant grandparents. For those who believe or want to believe in miracles, many will be touched by the stories that tell of visions and coincidences which we believe to be examples of God's intervention in a way we don't yet understand.

On the Way Home I Bumped into God is a gift that can fill our empty spaces, clear our confusion, offer hope, and ease the longing we have all experienced, for with this gift we can recognize and ponder when and why God has bumped into us on our own journey home.

MJG November, 2016

Note to the Reader

This book has been a collaborative effort which has drawn on the experiences and skills of our husband-and-wife team. The narration of events and personal relationships, as well as the commentaries and insights, have been prepared and included only after lengthy discussions which determined and shaped the message and character of the book. It would be impossible to accurately and separately account for our unique contributions. However, the voice you hear speaking in stories is mostly Ray's. Organizational designs and any epigraphs, commentaries, poetry, book chapter titles are usually Marion's.

This is not our first collaboration and, per usual, discussions regarding a multitude of issues were heated, sometimes to the point of challenging our wedding vows. However, the final product, with whatever inadequacies, flaws, or points of dispute a reader may discern, represents our combined best effort to explore and express our beliefs and to encourage others to explore and express theirs.

We would also like to acknowledge that we had some qualms about our presentation of the ideas contained in this book, for we know that often when developing the kind of ideas we are exploring here, there is the possibility that some might think that we feel we are uniquely capable of such exploration because we are, or have always been, in tune with how God works in our lives. This is absolutely not the case. In fact, the opposite is true, for we share the human capacity to stray from all that we know is right or good. Our intent here was simply to share our perception of how God attempts to extend His love and His grace to souls like us who are searching for His light and truth.

The book contains seven quotations from the Bible. Where such quotations occur they are cited, chapter and verse. The quotes all come from one version of the Bible. That version is, The Douay-Rheims Version of the Holy Bible (DRV), American Edition published in 1899.

MJG November, 2016

Introduction

But Not Really by Chance

I don't think of myself as a person who has trouble staying focused, but then maybe I just don't want to admit it. Actually, the issue of focus, especially when attending Mass has been bothering me for several years now. It really became obvious one day at the Saturday afternoon Mass Marion and I often attend. I can distinctly remember telling myself that the Consecration of the Mass would soon occur and that I should remain focused so as not to miss it. But, the next thing I remembered was the priest lifting the chalice. I said to myself, "What happened to the host—no host today?" The host is always elevated before the chalice. And then it hit me.

I had zoned out. The priest didn't miss raising the host. I did. I actually couldn't believe it because I had so carefully told myself to pay attention. So, there I was in church in the middle of the most important part of the Mass, and God couldn't capture my attention. And I am not a fidgety child or reluctant teen ager. I am an adult who loves the Mass.

I talked to my sister about this problem. She laughed, "You too? It happens to me all of the time." Then I thought to myself that maybe this inability to stay focused during the Mass was a family thing. But, as I talked to more and more friends, I found that such lack of attention was definitely not just a family problem.

What a task God has set for himself. He creates us and asks us to love Him and our fellow man, a task that requires knowledge, persistence, and commitment. But somehow either we just get distracted by the events or people in our lives, or we never really understood what we were supposed to be about. So, we live our lives rather superficially. We often miss the most important things—how to love others or appreciate how others have loved us. Even though we have memorized our catechism lessons, read the Bible, and studied the life of Jesus from his birth to his death on the cross, we still fail to pay attention to or act on the profound meaning these messages and events are attempting to convey to each of us. We attend Mass, give to charities, and even occasionally help our neighbors. But, obviously that isn't enough.

So, how does God get our attention? How does he get us to understand that just being at Mass, just occasionally handing a buck to a guy on the street corner, just reaching out to a stranger once in a while, or just helping a neighbor only when he is knocking on our door—though good things—are not enough? Knowing our weaknesses, how does he get in there and really get our attention.

That's what this book is all about. It's a book about the things God does to get our attention. Well, it's about how he got my attention. But as you read it, I am sure you will find these experiences very familiar, for how he gets me to look his way is probably not much different than the way he gets to you. I call it His back-up plan, for that is another thing about God I've come to understand: when he finds something that works, he tends to stay with it.

My experience with God's back-up plan is that it is multifaceted. Sometimes God has the people whom we admire tell us stories— stories that really move us. They are stories that reflect God's love, the beauty of giving, and the kindness of our fellow man like the story in this book titled, "The Christmas Purse." Or, God has us constantly bump into people who challenge us to do more—to be more—like the homeless man you will meet in "Brother, Can You Spare a Dime?," the factory laborer Jose, or the mission-filled college friend, Big Ed.

Other times, in order to get our attention, God just gets, as they say, "up close and personal," as in the story of my brother Joe holding a psychologically and physically wounded young man who weeps and longs for his lost innocence and the feel of a kind hand, or as He gifted me with the vision I experienced many years ago on a Wisconsin hill top.

Then there are stories about the times when God chose the perfect moment to place people in my life who, despite their human failures, taught me about strength, wisdom, compassion, and courage—people who were not remote heroes or medieval saints, but people who walked with me daily like my Busia (grandmother), or Lefty, Joe, or my childhood buddy, Bobby. These are people of my youth I will never forget. As you read about them and the gifts they gave me, I am sure they will remind you of your own heroes and saints, also never to be forgotten.

There are stories in this book which are humorous and light-hearted. I have included them, for I am sure that deeply embedded in God's nature is the capacity to be playful—a capacity captured in a line from one of my favorite movies, *Bagger Vance*: "They say that God is happiest when his children are at play." I thought that as you read, you might enjoy the respite of God's children at play.

Though most of the stories and events portrayed in this book are positive, evil also makes its appearance. It was—and is—a reality I could not ignore. Though I tried not to belabor the existence of evil, its occasional occurrence is, unfortunately, part of everyone's reality. It is disheartening to know that some people continue to make such dark choices, despite God's back-up plan, but in these stories, whether evil devastates a young boy, unjustly exploits laborers, or punishes those who are different from us, we see the capacity of people to respond with loving acts of comfort, support, and courage.

As I look back over my life, I see how God is a consummate lover. He never gives up. He wants our love so much that He just keeps at it. Time after time He comes at us. When He does get our attention, the experience often hits like a sledge hammer because it was so hard for Him to get our attention in the first place.

If He finally gets us to look into His eyes, He doesn't want us to forget that moment, like the time I saw His joyous reflection in the eyes of my daughter Tanya who returned home to her own safe and secure back yard after having had successful surgery. When she looked up at me in that sun-filled back yard, her smile was a beatific vision. If we are lucky, life provides us with a handful of such smiles.

It took seventy years of living to truly "get" the meaning of these experiences and to understand that I was meeting in those moments—not really by chance—the God we long and need to know.

RJG November, 2016

If the total number of human beings living on this planet could comfortably live together in one neighborhood as a family, who could possibly conceive that we could then watch one of our own die from lack of water to drink if we had enough water to flush our toilets, irrigate our lawns, or play in our pools? But, we live on a vast planet where not only don't we know our own neighbors; we don't even know the names of the countries from which many others come. Thus, we develop and maintain the foundations of human inequality, hoarding, and greed with no feeling of guilt. So how does a God of love jar our human sensitivities?

CHAPTER ONE

"Brother, Can You Spare a Dime?"

Our two oldest sons played football for Northwestern University. Marion and I and our youngest son Tom would often go to their home games in Evanston, Illinois. Because the university was some distance from our home, we would arrive the day before and stay at a hotel. Our favorite was the Orrington in downtown Evanston. Not only was it a lovely old hotel with a great deal of charm, it was within walking distance of the football stadium. It was perfect for us.

One very beautiful mid-October Friday, we left home and headed north to Evanston. We got there around 5:00 p.m. We went to our room, did a bit of unpacking, and then headed downstairs to the hotel restaurant for a quiet and lovely meal. We were in good spirits and the view outside of the restaurant window just added to the dinner pleasure. The trees on both sides of the street were ablaze with their fall colors, and the evening touches of sunlight were performing magic with their leaves. At meal's end, Marion decided that she wanted to go up to the room and rest a bit. Tom and I headed outdoors for an evening walk.

We found it to be a fairly busy evening for walkers with a lot of people rushing to get somewhere. We talked of football and other things and eventually, after going a fair distance, turned the corner at McDonald's where the sidewalk was fairly crowded.

Out of the corner of my eye, I caught sight of what appeared to be a homeless man near the McDonald's entrance. He had his left hand out and cupped, while with his right hand he held together his lightweight, tattered, and zipper-less jacket. He was very unkempt, and next to him on the ground was a bundle tied together at the top with a stick. He stood there unnoticed by virtually everyone—one of God's silent and invisible poor. Tom and I continued to walk and talk. I found myself drawn to and looking directly at the homeless man as his eyes locked unswervingly on me in a deep and profoundly peaceful way. He looked like someone I should know. I remember at that moment saying to myself, "Why not, I can afford a buck or two."

I knew I had given my wallet to Marion as she went to our hotel room, but I was sure I had some cash. I reached into my pocket and was pleasantly surprised. As I neared the homeless stranger, I pulled the cash out and looked into my right hand —a twenty dollar bill. I glanced at him; he smiled faintly then turned his head away, as if to deliberately discontinue our gaze and provide for me an option. I looked down at Tom. He didn't seem to know what was going on. I slowly and somewhat shamefully pocketed the money and Tom and I headed back toward the hotel. I remember affirming to myself:

"How can I give him a twenty? That's really too much. It's unreasonable. No one would expect me to give him a twenty."

I tried to calm a conscience that didn't want to be calmed.

After our short walk back, as we got near the hotel, I reached into my pocket, then stopped dead in my tracks. The money was gone. I looked down at Tom and without explaining to him said, "Quick, Tom, we have to go back."

I knew we wouldn't find the money. I had dropped it on the ground somewhere. But, I had to look. We turned around and double-timed it down the sidewalk. As we walked quickly, I could see through the half-crowded sidewalk ahead of us the homeless guy coming our way. As we neared him, I could see that he was looking at me and slowly waving his hand in the air. We came to within a few yards and then I could hear him saying, "Sir, Sir." I stopped. "Sir, Sir, you dropped this." Crumpled in his waving hand was my twenty dollar bill. He continued, "I found it right after you left, but couldn't keep up with you and the boy."

As I looked into his eyes, I remembered why I had been compelled to look his way in the first place. It was his eyes. They were so deep, peaceful and caring—so calm and gentle. They belied the rest of his appearance. His eyes were not homeless at all.

I felt so ashamed, so utterly unworthy. I was old enough and had lived long enough to know the inequities of this world. Yet, I had so quickly slid into the rationale of personal greed: "Why should I give generously to this beggar? I have worked hard for my share."

Finally and sheepishly, I said. "Sir, would you please keep the money? I would be honored if you would."

He replied, "Only if you really want me to."

"I do."

"Then I will, and bless you."

He smiled a very quiet and calm smile, looked again into my eyes, then turned and walked away. I took Tom back to the hotel and up to our room. Later I took a walk by myself. I looked for the man with eyes that seemed to calm me and bring me this strange peace. I could not find him. Those I asked said that they had not seen anyone such as I described—no one at all.

I never did find him. All I do know is that whoever he was, he was peacefully at home in our world. He was more at home than almost anyone I had ever met. He wasn't homeless at all. I began to think that maybe it's we who are the homeless and needy wanderers. Maybe it is we who have never truly understood God's life lessons—lessons that he teaches every day if we just listen and look.

"...Lord when did we see thee hungry and feed thee; thirsty and gave thee drink?"

Matthew 25:37

There is an arrogance that many of us are prone to have, especially those of us who are prosperous and powerful. We have somehow come to believe that we are in control. Sports announcers reflect this belief when they so often comment about a team's prospect for success, "They control their own destiny." But do they—do we— really control our own destiny? My assignment to the rolling mill was simply the result of being given the next job that needed to be filled. So, meeting Jose? Pure coincidence. Or was it? Are there really coincidences, or was I again being "bumped?" by God.

CHAPTER TWO

Jose and the Rolling Mill

In the late 1950s, at the age of 19, I began to work as a laborer at Inland Steel, one of the many steel mill plants built along the southern shores of Lake Michigan. No one could have prepared me for the experience.

After I disembarked the in-plant bus, walked through the locker room, and entered the rolling mill, I was overwhelmed. I couldn't believe that a facility built by man could be that big. On my left was massive machinery some 30 feet high and equally as wide—machinery that went on for hundreds of yards away from me into the perspective.

One hundred feet above my head, huge cranes with massive chains moved silently by. Each crane had, as its load, a 30-to-70 thousand pound steel coil. The coils were being moved to waiting trucks to be taken across the country. In front of me as far as I could see was an avenue of concrete nearly as wide as the length of a football field where workers scurried in all different directions. Everywhere I looked there were forklifts and vehicles of every type moving at various speeds, some loaded and some not. This vast collection of machines and humanity was covered by a huge dome of steel. While each of the machines made their own unique sounds, it was the incessant hum of the plant—an overwhelming sound—that flooded my senses and wouldn't let go.

It was lunch time on my third day on the job. I was working with a labor gang. The whistle had just blown. I had my lunch bucket under my arm and was taking my gloves off when I noticed I was near the loading dock. So I continued in that direction. As I approached, I saw a lone worker who had just made his way to the concrete lip of the dock and was now sitting and getting ready to eat. As I neared him, I stopped. He was familiar. I had seen him the day before, shoveling next to me.

I said, "Can I join you?"

He replied, "I not speak good English."

I said, "Neither do I."

He smiled and motioned me to sit. We talked that day of Mexican food, baloney sandwiches, and hostess cupcakes—nothing terribly profound. The next day we shared lunches, names, and a little about ourselves. His name was Jose; he was married, had three children, lived in the Harbor and had moved here from Mexico because where he had been born and had lived his whole life there were no jobs.

Over the weeks as we ate together on that dock we became friends. He had only gone to the third grade and was fascinated with schooling. He prodded me often about college, wanting to know as many of the specifics as I could tell him. His questions were endless: "What do you do in your classes?" "What do they talk about?" "If you don't know, are they patient with you?" "Are the books difficult?"

His enthusiasm and interest in knowing were profound. He had the eagerness and zeal of a young child. He reminded me much of my own father—the kind of a person who always wanted the window seat in an airplane so that even at age 70 he could still look out and see new things.

Though Jose and I were both in the same labor gang, we didn't often work together as there were many members who made up that group. On one occasion when we were paired, we were completing the day by sweeping down a large area where there had been a lot of activity. I remember thinking that we were finished and then noticed Jose going to the corner of the work area. I followed him to see what was going on. As I approached, I could see that he had placed his broom in the corner of the floor next to the concrete wall and was attempting to get the final, smallest pieces of dirt out of that corner area. I watched him for a while and then asked, "Jose, what are you doing? It's clean enough."

He looked up at me, smiled and said, "I do not clean this for them. It is for me. It is for Jose's pride."

When he was finished, we put our brooms over our shoulders and walked to the locker room. Since the time I worked with Jose, I have, over the years, worked with many people, both men and women. It has been rare for me to have had the privilege of working with people who had Jose's work ethic and sense of personal pride.

Lunch conversations for me became life lessons. Though Jose never intentionally tried to teach me, I learned a lot from him including some understanding of his culture. On one occasion he told me of a trip he had taken to Mexico several years earlier in order to see his father who was quite ill. He had gone by himself because of the cost. He had to walk the last several miles to his father's door. When he finally arrived, he knocked and the door was opened to him. Standing there in the doorway was his father. He said that he smiled. His father frowned and then slapped him firmly on the face and in Spanish said, "My son, where is your courtesy—remove your hat."

I remember being upset. Jose sensed it and immediately stopped me, "No, Ray, I had made the trip to my father but had not come far enough. I had forgotten the old ways. The old ways are his ways and they are good ways. They are honorable ways. They are not mine to rebuke. I removed my hat and apologized to my father. He smiled. We embraced. Then I embraced my mother. We shared a meal, then drank, laughed, and told stories of bygone times."

One of the jobs to which we were occasionally assigned was the individual inspection of sheets of steel. The relatively thin-gauged steel sheets were about three feet wide and five feet in length. They were always stacked and moved to a work station located near fork trucks. The location where I was working one day was near an exterior wall of the plant. I stood in front of a pile of these sheets, stacked about four feet high. Behind me was a temporary wall of various materials that had not yet been moved to a more permanent and appropriate location.

The job involved picking up the edge of the top sheet with a suction cup that was secured to my right hand and then shaking and lifting the entire sheet. Once it was lifted, I would hold the sheet in front of me, scan the sheet before a set of bright lights, and look for pin holes. The bright light behind the sheet that I held up would make the pin holes visible. If pin holes were found, I would place that sheet on a stack directly behind me. If there were no pin holes, the sheet would be placed on a stack to my left. Once I got the hang of the job, I found that it was, in fact, quite boring.

It was about 2:00 p.m. that day, and I had been at the work station since early morning, except for my half hour lunch break on the dock with Jose. At that moment, all I remember hearing was a rather loud sound from somewhere behind me. I began to turn to look, and then everything went black. The next thing I remember was that Jose was kneeling next to me as I lay on the ground. He had a tight grip on my right wrist, and as I opened my eyes I could see what appeared to be blood everywhere.

"It be okay, you lie still, you hurt. I have called for help, but do not be afraid. God sent me."

I simply nodded and then I couldn't seem to stay awake. The wall behind me had fallen directly on my head and shoved me into the sheets of steel. The edge of one of the top sheets cut across my wrist. The blood I saw everywhere was my own. Apparently, I had been without help for quite a few minutes, but while the blood loss was significant, it was not critical. It likely would have become critical had Jose not found me, for I was advised by the clinic doctors immediately after the incident that the cut I took came within one-sixteenth of an inch from severing the artery.

The following week Jose and I sat again on the dock wall and ate lunch. We ate in silence for several minutes, and then I broke the silence and asked, "Jose, why did you say to me when I was hurt that God sent you?"

He looked at me somewhat puzzled and said, "Because he did." Then he continued, "There was no reason for me to be there that day. I be there only because someone forget to bring enough shovels. We were short, and I said I would go back and get shovels. This never happens." He then smiled with a glimmer of joy in his eyes and concluded, "It was not your time and only He decides when that will be. So, He sent me." He then turned back to his sandwich, and we sat there and finished our lunch.

I had come to the mill that summer to make enough money to go back to college. I did not come to continue my studies while eating lunch on the concrete lip of the loading dock. But that's not what God had in mind.

The money I earned allowed the continuation of my studies, but that was the lesser of the treasures I took back to school with me. My pockets that summer had been filled with treasures of understanding—an understanding of the deeper and more profound values found in the souls, hearts and smiles of my fellow man. My additional formal education would be of value, but would not necessarily being me closer to my God.

I came to understand that it is the interactions with the Jose's of the world that most significantly help guide our confused path. They are a part of God's gift of continual nudging that keeps our path clear.

One of the treasured gifts from God was to be born the grandchild of immigrant peasants. Their gifts to me were penetrating clarity, deep faith, and simplicity. God was ever present in their lives. He was thanked by them for the food we ate, for the rain that nurtured the soil, for the gifts of one another, and for all things good. He was lovingly thanked with praise and in the simplest of ways—thanked with a gift of coins carried to church each Sunday by an immigrant peasant in her plain little handkerchief. It was all she had to give.

CHAPTER THREE

A Foot Still in the Old Country

Busia

The name that we affectionately used for her was "Busia," the word for grandmother in Polish. She was loved by all of her grandchildren and staying overnight at her home was always looked forward to with great delight. Those oldest of her grandchildren, like me and my brother Joe, stayed longer, sometimes for months at a time, during World War II and for a number of years after the war.

One of the treasures that Busia had on her property was a magnificent apple tree that Dziadzia (grandfather in Polish) had planted for her in 1935. It was a graceful tree with proper room to grow. Each summer it would bear wonderful fruit. Pies, canned apples, and apple butter came from that fruit.

I can remember seeing Busia angry only once. It happened on a warm, mid-summer day on the side of the house where that apple tree grew. My brother Joe and I had gotten into an apple-throwing war with two neighborhood kids that we had never before met. The warring weaponry was made up from the apples that had fallen to the ground from that very tree. When Busia saw us, she rushed out of the back side door. She was livid. It was an anger that neither Joe nor I had ever seen in her before. The two young warring strangers quickly ran and we were alone with her.

As she pointed her finger at us, shaking it repeatedly, we could see that her anger had brought her to tears. Our immediate assumption was that we had provoked her wrath as a consequence of fighting. But, we were wrong. Through her broken English and anger we were hearing and understanding something very different. We, her grandsons, had been abusing a gift of food that God in his goodness had given to her and her family. She was ashamed and disgraced.

She picked up some of the battered apples lying on the ground, brushed off the dirt and gently placed them into her apron. Still sobbing, she then turned from us and slowly walked back into the house. She left us there feeling a shame we had never before felt.

Every year I had watched her faithfully plant and tend her garden and her fruit trees. I had even assisted her with the plants, pulling the weeds and hoeing the soil. But until we had seen her express such anger, neither I nor my brother Joe had understood what her garden meant to her. For her, this growing, nurturing, and eventual harvesting was not just a way of life, it was a daily communion with her God. Each plant and each tree was an act of faith that would bring a response in the form of a harvest—a response promised to an old Polish peasant who understood and cherished this bond. With her pointing finger, she was attempting to share with her grandsons the meaning and depth of this communion.

The next spring as Joe and I helped her plant her garden, we saw her do things that we had never noticed before. She spoke quietly to the seeds and the new sprouts. She tended to the soil around them ever so gently, noticing where additional soil might be needed or pressed more firmly. As weeks went by and we moved with her along the rows of plants, we could see that she knew each one, even anticipating what their needs might be. We were seeing things that we had never seen before—perhaps because we had been too young, perhaps because of something else?

In the late summer and fall, the harvesting of her trees and plants was done in the manner of one accepting gifts from someone of whom you are very fond. During those times, she often hummed the tunes I believe that she carried to this land from her home in Poland so many years before. I think they were probably tunes she had hummed as she assisted with the harvestings or as she walked through those meadows tending the animals.

In a very sad sense, I have not, since my experiences with Busia, spent my life with farmers. As I grow older, I wish I had, like my brother Joe, done so. I'm not sure that any of us should ever get too far from the soil or from the peasants who spend their lives tending to it in simple harmony with their God.

The Saw Sharpener

Most old country neighborhoods had a saw sharpener. My Dziadzia was that craftsman. During the day, he built boxcars for trains in his work place. In early evenings and on Saturdays in his back yard he sharpened saws. He was well-known throughout the neighborhood as one who prided himself in his work, so he was never without work. There was always a handful of saws waiting their turn.

As with all artisans, his tools were trustworthy and simple. The real skills needed to do a fine job were, however, not in his tools. Rather, they were in the experienced feel of the hands and arms of this craftsman.

Joe and I, and in later years my sister Barbara, always liked to watch him set up his work. The wooden saw horse that securely held the saw being worked on was the centerpiece of the crafting endeavor. It had its place in the back yard several feet from the wood pile.

The many and various files that Dziadzia used in his work were not kept in the shed in the backyard, but rather in the basement. They were tools he wished to protect from the outdoor moisture and seasonal temperature changes. As he considered the work needed to sharpen a saw, he would first take that saw into the basement and then carefully choose the files he wanted. He would take these files and the saw back outside to the wooden saw horse.

The saw horse had an enclosed wooden pocket at chest level. It was here that he would put the files that he had selected to use in the sharpening of the saw. In addition, the saw horse had a two-by-four section of wood fastened about a foot off the ground and parallel to it so that he could rest his right or left foot as he moved his hands and file in a rhythm across the teeth of the saw.

For a reason I never clearly understood, he seemed to most enjoy his work sharpening saws during the warmest part of summer afternoon days. Perhaps in that situation he was less pained by an arthritis that had plagued him long before he was what one might call an old man. I can picture him still in the back yard near his wood pile in the full sun. He always donned a baseball cap and wore a long-sleeved white undershirt with and a red neckerchief around his neck.

He would start out by placing his left foot up on the two-by-four. Then with the file placed properly in his hands, he would slowly move the file back and forth. Sometimes, like a golfer following through on his swing, he would lift the file off of the saw as he came to the end of a movement. Eventually, after many such passes, his entire body would flow in a wave-like motion— to and fro, to and fro.

With heavier files the motion would be slower, and he would exert more pressure. Before he was finished, he turned his attention to each tooth of the saw and then his technique would always be gentler and more relaxed and the files used would be the smallest and most delicate.

He kept a pint of Seagram's in his right back pants pocket, and by the end of a long afternoon two or three saws would have experienced the master's touch and the pint would be no more.

The three of us would often sit on the grass in front of him as he worked. We would be mesmerized by the rhythmic, shrill, steel-on-steel symphony of sounds. He would, on those days, talk to us as he worked and ask us to note the differences in the sounds as the files did their work with each tooth. Eventually and predictably, he would explain to us in his Polish not only what was happening to the saw, but what we could learn from it:

"The hard work that the saw has done over time has changed it. It has lost its harmony. The work of the files brings that harmony back. Listen now to how the sound of the file and the sound of the saw are becoming one. When that sound becomes one and the scratch is no more, then the tooth of the saw is good. When all of the teeth have the sound of one, the saw is good—it is again in harmony. For the carpenter, new work with the saw can once again be a work of joy. With your lives, find the things that have lost their harmony. Help them to come back and this will bring you joy."

Then he would smile at us, pull out his tobacco pouch from his shirt pocket, roll one of his own, lean back on his bench and after lighting, exhale smoke slowly into the summer sky. In later years, as we reflected on his words, we understood he was talking to us of more than the harmonies of the saw.

The ways and manners of Busia and Dziadzia were gentle and graceful nudges sent by God. The simplicity of how they lived their lives was elegant. They slowly and patiently breathed in their lives in harmony with their God and then as patiently and lovingly exhaled it upon us. All we had to do was to breathe it in.

Like most of the Catholic kids I grew up with, I was always enamored of the pictures and stories surrounding Michael the Archangel. What a hero he was to head up the multitudes of good angels and crush Lucifer and his posse of evil! He recognized evil and went after it. God did not suggest that he turn the other cheek—just move in there with righteous indignation and whack away.

This was my childhood understanding of Lefty.

CHAPTER FOUR

Lefty

He was my dad. I didn't know his Christian name was John until I was 14 and graduating from grade school. No one ever called him John. As I grew older, I learned from Lefty that those of us fortunate enough to be alive are either eating our way through life, or being eaten by it. Lefty ate. He took big bites and then leaned back and roared with a laughter that came from way down deep. In his private moments he quietly hummed or sang the songs from the 20s and 30s that he loved.

I remember one occasion where I was supposed to pick him up at a golf course. As I was on my way to the course, I was driving into the jaws of a full-blown thunderstorm with heavy winds coming off of Lake Michigan. When I finally got to the course, I couldn't see a thing. I got out of the car and, with my hands cupped over my forehead, tried to see onto the course. It was useless. Then through that vicious storm, I could hear faint whistling coming from somewhere down the first fairway. As I stood there with the storm obscuring almost everything, I began to see a foursome of golfers marching, shoulder to shoulder, on their way to the clubhouse. They marched to the tune that famously introduced the opening scene of the movie "The Bridge over the River Kwai," while thunder, rain and lightning surrounded them. It was Lefty and his steel mill buddies. Like I said—big bites.

He had a magnetic personality. People just liked him—people of all kinds. As I grew up, I found that he loved back. First he loved his God, then his wife, others he considered family and, finally, the rest of mankind—in that order.

He had grown up during the height of the Great Depression and had frequently experienced prolonged hunger. He was, during those years, a valedictorian, a Golden Gloves Champion in Chicago, and a semi-pro football player. He turned down scholarships for wrestling at the University of Iowa and football at Indiana University. Instead, he secured work in the steel mills of the lower Great Lakes. For 40 years he would make steel, then fill the molds and ladles with the molten steel that came from his Open Hearth furnace. For most of his adult working life he would suffer severe and chronic back pain, needing often to be carried from the mill at the end of a shift. But he always returned for the next shift, if such was his duty. He would often say of his work, "I owe them a full, honest day's work; they owe me a living wage. I cannot be responsible for their part of the bargain, only my part."

What he most abhorred in life was unfairness. When he perceived injustice, his aggressive personality would take over and out would come the sword of Michael and he would be into the fray.

In much earlier times, Edmond Burke wrote the following in a letter to Thomas Mercer, "The only thing necessary for the triumph of evil is for good men to do nothing." Edmond would have enjoyed Lefty.

An Old Friend

One of my earliest significant memories of Lefty took place when I was about five years old. We were in my grandfather's back yard. Dad was searching for several two-by-fours as he was doing some carpentry work in our upstairs apartment down the street. I was sitting on the top of the five-foot high wood pile—a favorite kid's spot. We were talking.

"Dad, I got a new friend."

"Really, who is it?"

"Well, you know across the street from our house, past the brick yard and close to the coal yard?"

"Yeah."

"Well, there's a black kid there my size. We played last night and I like him. His uncle from Chicago came by when we were playin' and asked me who I was. I told him and he wanted to know if I was Lefty's kid. I told him I was. Then he said he had played football with you and that you and he had been good friends—told me to tell you that Charlie said hello. You remember him?"

"Sure do. Haven't seen Charlie in years—liked him a lot. Charlie and I did play football together, and we grew up together in this same neighborhood."

"Tell me about him, Dad."

"He may have been the fastest kid I have ever known. But more importantly on a football field he could change directions as he ran without losing speed."

"Is that good, Dad?"

"It sure is, Ray. If we had just given him the ball every time, and had me and other guys block for him, our team would have gone undefeated. We never would have lost a game."

"Did they give him the ball every time?"

"No."

"Why?"

"Because he was black."

"I don't understand, Dad."

"Ray, just because you're the best, doesn't mean that the world is going to give you the chances you deserve. Charlie didn't get the ball often at all. I remember one time in practice, he was carrying the ball and ran up the middle for a great gain and then lots of players piled on him. When my brother Walt and I got over to the pile, we could hear Charlie screaming from underneath. We started pulling guys off. When we got to Charlie, we could see that he had huge bite marks all over his legs and arms. We pulled him up to his feet and he stood there between Walt and me, shaking from shock and pain."

"His own teammates, Dad?"

"Yeah, his teammates."

"What did you do?"

"Right there on that field with Charlie between us, we told those guys that if anything like that ever happened again to Charlie, we would come into their neighborhood, find them, and whether they were alone or in a group, beat the shit out of them right on the street in the presence of their neighbors and families."

"Did you do it?"

"Didn't have to."

"Why?"

"It never happened again."

"Why?"

"They knew we meant it."

Dad then stopped his lumbering work and just stared for a long moment quietly in the direction of our apartment and the coal yard beyond. Then he said, "Son, come on off of that wood pile. We can do this job later. Right now, God willing, there is an old friend visiting some of his family, and he and you deserve a proper introduction."

Later that afternoon Dad introduced me to an old friend. I said hello, shook hands, and then went off with my new friend to play in the brick yard. Dad and Charlie just sat on the front steps of an old house nearest the coal yard. They sat there a long time, just talking and drinking a couple of beers. I think if God were looking down at that moment He would have liked what he saw.

There is a movie that I am very fond of. It is titled *Gentleman's Agreement*. In the movie John Garfield, who plays an American Jewish military officer, is at dinner with Dorothy McGuire who plays Kathy Lacey. Kathy laments to John about how sick she felt when a party guest at a recent dinner told a joke that demeaned Jews. Dave repeatedly asks her what she did about it. She, of course, did nothing and now feels ashamed.

There are certain habits most of us are encouraged to develop during our childhood—habits like cleaning up after ourselves, or saying thank you to someone who is kind to you, or being respectful of our elders. I think there is another habit that should be taught—the habit of responding to injustice. We need to be "bumped," as it were. Kathy had not developed that habit. Lefty had, and to be raised in his presence meant those of us who lived with or near him periodically received a bump we would always remember.

Pea Shoot

Not every job in the steel mill was a killer. Second-helper of an open hearth furnace was. You worked yourself up from the labor gang to third-helper and then to second-helper where you stayed for the next ten to fifteen years. You answered directly to the boss of the furnace—the first-helper. His job was primarily cognitive, yours was physical. Your shovel was your best friend, and you kept the metal end of it sharp.

In one eight-hour shift you might shovel as much as 20 tons of various metals into wheelbarrows, so you needed to minimize any friction at the end of your shovel. If it was hot, over 110 degrees—130 near the furnace—and you had been shoveling for over four hours, that sharpened edge could make the difference between suffering through the last four hours from non-stop cramping, or just enduring intermittent cramping that you could tolerate until you heard the end-of-shift whistle.

There were no overweight second-helpers. You could always pick them out in the locker room. They were chiseled. If they left the day's work clothes in the locker, those clothes could easily be spotted. They were the ones stiff and white with salt. Second-helpers were also identifiable because they were the ones who drank as much water as they could at the beginning of the shift and took as many salt tablets as they could tolerate.

Because of their necessary proximity to the furnace itself, second-helpers were often burned by the marble-sized molten iron pellets that rained down on them after the furnaces spewed the pellets into the air. These little pieces of molten steel would cut through a man's shirt as they rained down. Then they would cut lines along his wet back all the way to his waist. If the molten pellets got lodged in the belt area, it was real trouble as they could leave holes in the skin and outer muscles of the back. Then, as that man sweated in the days that followed, salt from the sweat would get into those holes causing great pain.

I was nine years old when I first saw my dad without a shirt. He was coming out of the bathroom heading for his bedroom and I saw the fresh red raw wounds on his back. I remember that I wanted to cry. He saw me, got down on one knee and immediately tried to comfort me. He seemed to know how upset I was and said with a smile, "It's okay, son." He talked to me for a long time. But it wasn't okay. I never again saw his back like that because I never again saw him shirtless. But he was a second-helper for the next 11 years, and during all of those years I knew he was suffering from those kinds of burns. I prayed a lot for him during those years, I prayed to God to not make it hurt so bad.

After 20 years as a steelworker, Lefty got his own Open-Hearth Furnace—No.33 plant—No. 2. He had some authority in the choice of his crew and picked Pea Shoot as his second helper. When WWII broke out, Lefty, like many young Americans, wanted to join the service. But he was 27, married, a father, a steelworker, and unable to pass the vision test. Pea Shoot, on the other hand, enlisted and got in right away. Pea Shoot served over four years and was not discharged until the war was over. He served in the Navy. He fought in nine major battles, some of which included attacks by Kamikaze pilots and he fought in an endless number of lesser battles as well. By war's end, he had a pocket full of ribbons and medals, but could not sleep without enduring the "sweats" and having constant nightmares. And, sadly, he had become an alcoholic. Lefty knew all of this when he took him on, but he took him on anyway. Lefty liked him. But more than that, he saw Pea Shoot as someone we owed. For the remainder of his life he looked at all vets that way—people we owed.

Lefty's dad, my grandfather, was an alcoholic and a mean, sometimes violent one, so when Lefty took on Pea Shoot he knew all about what he might be getting into. And much of what he anticipated came to pass. But he never quit on him, even when Pea Shoot didn't show for work and Lefty had to cover for him, or even when his wife would call at four o'clock in the morning, and Lefty would have to go find him in some Indiana Harbor bar or in the alleyway behind it. He never quit.

On only one occasion did he talk to me about Pea Shoot. It was over some beers at the kitchen table after a 4 to 12 shift. We talked to first light. What I remember most of that conversation was when he said to me, "Ray, Pea Shoot would give his right arm gladly and shovel the rest of his life only with the use of his left arm if he could beat this alcohol thing. That's how hard it's got a hold of him." In my adult life I worked for many years with addicts. I never forgot what Lefty said that night. That insight and need for empathy served me well on many occasions.

I remember the afternoon that Lefty got the call from Pea Shoot's wife. Pea Shoot was dead. The Police in East Chicago had found him in an alleyway in the Harbor. He hung up the phone and went with my mom to his bedroom. Dad never cried much but he did that day. He loved Pea Shoot and Pea Shoot had loved him. If God loved Pea Shoot only half as much as he was loved by my dad, then somewhere at that long table set in heaven for us all, there was a spot saved for Pea Shoot near the head.

I Work with Those Guys

Summers were often good times for our family. Occasionally, we would wake early, drive to the Dunes on Lake Michigan and picnic. Other times we might drive to a state park such as Starved Rock in Illinois and walk trails until our legs felt like they were going to fall off. There were also the pitch-in meals at the homes of extended family with baseball games in the street. As I said, summers were often good times for our family—except one time.

We had driven that morning to the house of a brother of one of our relatives. They lived near Chicago which was a bit of a distance. Nearly everyone arrived about noon. In our case, 8:45 Mass had been the day's first stop. When we arrived for the family pitch-in, we all helped mom bring the food she had prepared into the house, and then with baseballs, mitts, and bats we headed for the street. Over the next several hours we played, came in and out for food and drinks and took breaks on the grass near the curb. Then at about three-thirty in the afternoon, Mom came running out of the house screaming for me and Joe, "Go into the basement and get your father quick. It looks like there is going to be a fight."

Joe and I rushed to the house and through the side door which gave entry to the basement. We encountered Lefty on his way up the stairs. His white shirt was torn exposing part of his chest, and his tie, though still on his neck, was hanging down his back. He looked up as he reached the top step.

"Dad, are you okay?"

He responded. "Yeah, but they're not. Don't go down there."

It wasn't long before we were all in the car and on our way home. Mom, now sobbing, asked, "Lefty, how could you? Couldn't you let it go just this one time? They're family."

Lefty quietly responded. "Family, my ass!" Then he said nothing more. He just drove. It was a very quiet ride home.

It wasn't until sometime later that we were told what happened. Apparently after a number of beers and shots, several distant relatives got into a discussion about who in America worked the hardest. The conversation quickly took an ethnic and racial turn. Soon the focus became specifically blacks and their laziness and shiftlessness. Despite Lefty's strenuous objections and his warnings, they refused to change the conversation or focus. Their laughter and prodding actually got more intense.

The relatives had not understood the dead-end road they were heading down. However, Joe and I, upon hearing the story, immediately recognized that the outcome had been totally predictable, for Lefty worked with a lot of black guys. They were his friends, and he had learned over the years that he could count not only on their work ethic, but also on their support in hard times. What's more, he had warned the relatives to drop it and they hadn't. No one left in that basement that day had to be hospitalized, but apparently that had been a judgment call. We never got invited back.

"Do not think that I came to send peace upon the earth; I came not to send peace, but the sword. For I came to set a man at variance against his father, and the daughter against her mother, and the daughter-in-law against her mother-in-law."

Matthew 10:34-35

A Worthy Gift

During my early childhood, if a Catholic wanted to go to Communion at Mass it meant that he would have to fast — neither eating food nor drinking water from midnight the night before. The Apostolic Constitution of Pope Pius XII, "Christus Dominus," easing these rules didn't take place until 1953. And the fuller effect of all such rule changes did not take place until the early 1960s. For me, the most difficult part of these earlier rule obligations was watching my father painfully struggle because of them.

In the summers Lefty often had to work midnights and weekends because the assignment of work shifts was based in large part on seniority, and in those years he didn't have much seniority. So, from midnight Saturday through Sunday at 8:00 a.m., he was working a second-helper shift. The temperature in the plant those nights near the hot sides of the furnaces could run anywhere from the 90 to 110 degrees. In order to go to Communion at the 8:45 a.m. Mass, he had to forego water from the beginning of that shift until he left the 8:45 a.m. Mass the next morning. He would shovel manganese and other metals all through those nights and, as the end of the shift approached, he would shovel even more intensely in order to help the day shift get a head start on the busiest part of the day.

His cramps those mornings in church were intense and frequent. Tears from the pain would often run down his face. Out of the corner of my eye, I could see him near the center of our pew struggling unsuccessfully to straighten his limbs. Yet, he wouldn't leave the church or the pew that he sat in. To me, time seemed to drag, and the Mass felt like it was several hours long. I hated it. Finally, one day when I was about 11 years old, I asked him toward the end of Mass. "Why, Dad, why?"

He understood my concern and confusion. He sat next to me in the pew and said, "Son, I am not a perfect man. In my life I make many mistakes. As hard as I try, I still do the wrong thing many times. Just ask your mother." He smiled. "This thing that I do without food or water, having worked in the heat all night, is a gift to me from my God. He has given me a way to give back to him with my greatest capacity—my physical strength. Even though I struggle with it, it cleanses me, and I find it gives me a sense of worth and dignity. Son, I would have it no other way. I am just a man, and I know no other way. Do you understand?"

"I think so, Dad, I think so." With both of his hands on my shoulders, he looked at me and smiled.

As I gazed into his eyes, I understood. He was in love with his God and his giving in this way allowed him a deeper bond with his Creator. I found, as I continued to look at him that I envied him. He was not a perfect man, but I don't know that I have ever met one. All I do know is that he was a warrior and tried throughout his life to fight his best fight.

I would understand later that it was the habits that he had forged early in his life that sustained him. He would say his Polish Angel Prayer at day's end on his knees at the edge of his bed and he would always attend his Sunday Mass regardless of inclement weather or other inconveniences. He had the deepest respect for what he understood to be the face of his God.

Lefty was a long time member of the Knights of Columbus. He had never purchased the sword that comes with achieving the fourth-degree status. So, before he died, we bought one for him. He smiled and seemed pleased. Finally at age 93 he died and we buried that sword with him. It seemed quite appropriate, for where would it be better laid than by his side?

There are times when our encounters with God are neither mystical nor accidental—times when we ask for God's help in all the ways that tradition has taught us. With rosary beads, candle lights, solemn hymns, and simple prayers, we turn to Him for strength, hope, and comfort. War is such a time.

CHAPTER FIVE

War Remembered

I was born in 1940. I was my parents' second child. We lived in a one-bedroom, second floor apartment across from the coal yard on the western edge of the Polish ghetto in Hammond, Indiana. My parents' first child, my older brother, died shortly after his birth while my father, without health insurance, pleaded with the hospital to admit and take care of my mother. These were the hardest of times for our family and also for many of the nation's really poor. No one could tell those people that the depression was over, because for them it wasn't.

By the time our country entered the war, Dad had secured work at Inland Steel in East Chicago on the southern edge of Lake Michigan. He was a hard worker, and by 1941 at the age of 27, he was promoted to third-helper and assigned to one of the many open hearth furnaces that made up the massive steel-making plants. As the war progressed, we saw less and less of him for the production of steel had become one of our nation's top priorities.

During the war years, most of the extended-family activities took place in the homes of my grandparents. They were the oldest members of our American family, having migrated to the

United States in the early part of the century. They had come as children. My father's father made the journey alone at age 14— my mother's mother at age 19. Like so many other immigrants, they met their prospective spouses in the Polish ghettos that were expanding or coming into existence in different parts of America.

Most immigrants secured the best work they could find which for men usually meant unskilled labor jobs and for women, housework for wealthier families. Then, with the help of friends and their community, they constructed their churches and their homes. When World War II came, these homes, in addition to their churches, became the hearths where their families gathered to pray for the relatives and friends who had gone to serve in foreign lands and to share information about the progress of the war.

I remember how my own family members, often joined by neighbors, would gather in the homes of my grandparents. I can recall vividly the inevitable evening talks about my uncles and neighborhood friends who were now in faraway places with strange names, fighting an enemy that the youngest of us did not know.

In the evenings, families would often gather to hear the letters that came from those in the war. These were precious possessions which would be shared with those who were hoping to find that their loved ones were safe and in good spirits. Before the letters were read, a family prayer would be offered. This prayer, said aloud in Polish, was usually led by a grandparent or one of the older children. Then the letters would be read, reread, and even taken to other homes where they would be shared with other relatives and neighbors.

In addition to the sharing of letters, radio broadcasts sent by short-wave from England and other European countries were listened to. Those present, filled with anxiety, would listen quietly and carefully to news of the progress of the war. After such broadcasts, more prayers would be said, and then conversations in Polish would begin. These conversations would include translations of the news from the broadcasts and they would often take on a lighter tone, especially for the purpose of comforting the grandmothers (Busias) who sat in the center of such gatherings, clenching their rosaries and hoping for some relief from their constant fear.

It was difficult in those days to escape the undercurrent of fear and anxiety that always seemed to grip us. Even the early evening neighborhood walks that I so often took with my grandmother were filled with apprehensiveness and trepidation. As we walked, our conversations took place with porch-sitting neighbors, many of whom had displayed in their windows the blue star celebrating the fact of their son's or daughter's participation in the war. Conversations with these neighbors might cover an array of things, but it always included talk of the war and their children who were among the soldiers who were fighting in unknown and dangerous places, and it always included requests for continual prayers to be offered. "Don't forget to pray for Andy, or Eddie, or Johnny, or..." would always be added to an anxious good-by.

The most terrifying moments for me on those evening walks were to see that the blue star I had observed the previous day in a neighbor's window had been stitched over with gold cloth, indicating that their young soldier had been killed. I was always terrified to raise my eyes as I passed the houses of neighbors where I knew such blue stars were displayed. The fear that I would now see a gold star was overwhelming. I believe that those were my earliest childhood memories of terror.

The only relief from that terror would come from the night prayers I shared with Busia. She would often light the little candle at the base of the Blessed Virgin shrine on the dresser in the bedroom and then we would pray, first for those fighting in foreign lands and then for us at home. She would sit on the edge of my bed while I knelt. We would always conclude with the Angel Prayer in Polish. Its rhythm and harmony were always comforting. As she kissed me on the forehead, I could sense God and his angels nudging me into bed and saying, "It will be all right now. Sleep and dream of good things."

When the war ended, it did not end with a few shouts of cheer. Churches that were well-attended during the war overflowed with faithful parishioners and, I suspect, many non-believers. At Saint Mary's, votive candles blazed at the foot of the statues, especially the one of the Blessed Virgin Mary. The church never seemed to be empty. It was impossible to find a seat, and it seemed that the church bells rang forever. I can remember people, in those first days after the war, hugging each other for such a long time and with an intensity that I had never seen.

At war's end, few in my family seemed able to sleep. They simply stayed awake by themselves, or they talked, prayed, and laughed together into the late night hours. My bedroom opened onto the side of the living room, so I could listen until dawn to the quiet and warm conversations that went on there and even in the kitchen. When the young men and women in their uniforms came home to the family, the celebrations intensified and continued. It is difficult to relate my childhood memories of the total joy I observed in the whole community of adults in those days. The dancing, the singing in their broken English, and the visions of their total relief I still carry with me today, so very many years later.

It was not until years later that I understood the deeper reasons for the depth of fear that gripped these immigrants during the war. The Europe that they had left as children had often been a place of unspeakable evil. As children, they had seen and many times experienced horrible atrocities. They had observed the growth and development of the war machines in Europe. They had been told about or watched first-hand how quickly a person, an entire family, or a village could be crushed. They knew of the interrogations and disappearances—the overnight vanishing of friends and neighbors. They felt and lived that terror. They left their homes not just for the hope of better economic opportunities, they left for the safety and civilization America promised.

So, when the war began for their America, they blessed their children born in this new land as they watched them go off to this war, but their personal knowledge of war made them especially fearful that they would never see their children again. They did not understand or believe in the strength of this country's war machine. They were convinced that the war could only be won with their constant prayers. In the end the war was won, but in their minds the victory had little to do with our planes, and tanks, and ships. The winning, rather, was the result of praying the rosary, lighting little candles, singing solemn hymns, and saying millions of simple prayers. Until their deaths they could not be convinced otherwise.

I am not sure they were right, but who can really say they were wrong? I do know that the prayers they offered, alone and together, provided the comfort, hope, and strength they needed to survive the constant terror they felt. That was the lesson about the power of prayer I learned as a child while I lived among them. It is a lesson I carry with me even today.

"O grant us help from trouble: for vain is the help of man. Through God we shall do mightily: and he will bring our enemies to nothing."

Psalm 107:13

"At that hour the disciples came to Jesus, saying: 'Who thinkest thou is the greater in the kingdom of heaven?' And Jesus called unto him a little child, set him in the midst of them and said: 'Amen I say to you, unless you become converted, and become as little children, you shall not enter into the kingdom of heaven.'"

Matthew 18:1-3

CHAPTER SIX

God's Special Places Made for Little Children

In 1946 my sister Barbara was born. I remember thinking that she was the prettiest baby I had ever seen. As she grew older, she looked even prettier. Her shoulder-length hair was blonde, and she always wore pretty little dresses. Her smile seemed to come from way down deep—from some place of warmth and calm. Dad made it clear to Joe and me that whenever she was in our care playing outside, our first duty was to watch and protect her. We understood the gravity of that rule.

Near the end of the war, we moved from our Polish haven. The distance to work for Dad was taxing to say the least. We had no car and his walks to the bus stop were over three miles. In the middle of winter this was especially hard on him. My parents decided to move to the town of Hessville, a location that resolved the problem. We lived three houses from its western edge, and we traded the coal yard next to our East Hammond dwelling for the railroad tracks with the constant noise from the moving trains that shook our two-bedroom house and all the structures around. In the evenings and nights you could hear the constant high-pitched, steel-on-steel sounds coming from the roundhouse only three blocks away as tracks were switched for the early morning locomotive runs to locations all over the country.

Though Hessville and East Hammond were parts of the same broader community, there were for us kids many differences, especially in the languages we heard everywhere. It was strange not to hear adults speaking their foreign tongues. In East Hammond on nearly every block there were corner grocery stores, occasionally a butcher shop, and, of course, bars. In all of these establishments both business and casual conversations were usually conducted in a language other than English. Front porches were everywhere, and in the evening neighbors and friends paused or stopped for a brief or extended conversation, most often conducted in Polish. We were constantly listening to Polish, but also heard Yiddish, Russian, and Hungarian as well as several less common foreign tongues. In Hessville, we heard only English. This was, for us, the most striking difference.

Adjacent to the homes in our area, running the length of the railroad tracks, were the high tension electrical wires. They were held up by their enormous sixty-foot steel structures that looked like a parade of giant robots to our young minds. The area beneath these colossal steel structures ran from the tracks to the street bordering our community. It seemed to be an endless field where trees, bushes, prairie grasses, animals of all sorts, spiders, and all manner of bugs, bees, beetles and hornets made their homes.

We affectionately christened this area "The Weeds." Parental instructions permitted playing in The Weeds, but we were cautioned to avoid their western boundary—the railroad tracks.

Of course this would have been like saying to Adam and Eve, "don't eat of the beautiful fruit bearing tree, just play with the bugs." It, of course, didn't take long for Joe and me to visit the "forbidden lands" and eventually, with great trepidation, take our little sister Barbara. We would have probably even taken our youngest brother John, but at that time he was a babe in a crib. His time would come.

In days long past, Hammond and Hessville had small bodies of water known as the "Five Finger Lakes." Years and years of building houses, factories, roads, and land fill projects had all but eliminated the existence of these pristine Finger Lakes and the flora and fauna that surrounded them. Everything in this area had been eliminated except for one fairly small forgotten place— thirty to thirty-five acres of land beyond the tracks. It was now a land known only to the locomotive engineers and switchmen as they caught glimpses of this area while peering out of the windows of their trains which were moving at slower speeds toward the roundhouse and to the adventuresome children who ventured over the tracks and into these forbidden lands. Any child who explored this place shared a view of a scene that our American forefathers and their families must have found in every part of this virgin country before man conquered and civilized the wilderness.

Often as we peered down from the elevated railroad tracks, the small Finger Lakes glimmered back at us as the sunlight caressed the water's mostly calm surfaces. In our minds we were looking at God's special places made for little children.

The trees in and around the lakes were larger than the trees of The Weeds. The prairie grass flowers were of a wider array and their colors were more intense. As we approached, animals that had been comfortably sunning left their resting places and dove for the protection of the waters. The little lakes were clear and at their deepest points were four or five feet deep. Along the edges were hundreds of tadpoles of various sizes. The sand along the lakes was white beach sand, for this area had in its distant past been the shore of Lake Michigan.

There are thousands and thousands of these little treasure spots across our country. They are missed or forgotten by most adults. We see a muddy pond, or a dirty, wet place at the end of the railroad tracks. But the eyes of little children see a gift, a treasure. They see a place that calls to them to come, splash, touch, and play. They see with their clear and innocent eyes, as did my gentle sister, a little place that only God and they know about.

I think that God knew that not all children would have parents with the means to take them to the world's wondrous places, so he created these little sacred places everywhere—places that even the poorest child would somehow find, and then with Him, treasure this holy space.

Though Joe and I were always captivated by this scene regardless of the number of times we came, it was our little sister who seemed most taken. As she looked up from a bare-footed squatting position at the edge of the water, her smile seemed its most profound. At such moments I would invariably hear her ask, "Ray, is this one of God's favorite places?" "Yes it is, Barb," I would assure her. Then she would say, "I knew it, I knew it, I knew it. It's mine too," and with her small hand and child's fingers, she would gently, slowly, and quietly stroke the water and watch the tadpoles scurry and swim to different places—places I'm sure that only she and God talked about.

...."*Revenge is mine saith the Lord.*"

Romans 12:19

CHAPTER SEVEN

But Water Runs Through It

In 1946 Dad bought a 1937 Buick Opera Coupe. It was built like a truck. The gauge of the steel had to approximate the American tanks built shortly thereafter for the War. He loved that car and kept it often in the garage that he, his brothers and father had built in our back yard using mostly scrap lumber from Pullman Standard's refurbished train box cars.

When he was not at work and his car was not in the garage, he would put it in the back yard where he could perform any number of operations on it. These operations included, but were not limited to, oil changes, carburetor adjustments, spark plug repair, brake adjustments, wheel alignments, replacing kingpins and brake linings. These sessions were always capped off with washings and simonize treatments. Like I said, he loved that car.

The only real defect of the car was its extensive underbelly rusting and a number of subsequent holes in various places of the floor—a consequence of having been driven for so many years in the East Chicago area where salting the snowy and ice-covered streets in winter was necessary. In winter the cold air coming up from the icy street through the less than complete floor made the car's heater useless. This didn't bother him though, for Dad was one of the old breed known for their toughness. But, Mom always took a blanket to cover herself and Barbara, and in later years, my youngest brother John. Dad just grinned and, dressed in his normal attire, just drove on.

The back seat of the car was made up of two small "opera seats." They each had a steel rod at their base that was intended to rest on a small metal plate on the floor and thus be level and function as viable seats. The plates had long ago busted through, however, so Joe and I had to sit in the back seat area on less than level cushions. We would look down and watch through the floor holes as the streets went by underneath our feet.

In warm, spring, rainy weather, water would spray up into the back seat if Dad drove too close to the curb where rain run-offs accumulated on the street—sometimes in large pools of significant length. One learned quickly not to sit, under those conditions, behind the driver's seat, for that's where the tsunami would hit. Those were the days when Joe and I would rush for the car and fight for the passenger side rear seat. Our short struggle would usually result in our squeezing together into that seat.

I can remember on one particularly very rainy spring day, Dad, Joe, and I were finishing a visit at Dad's parents' home on the north side of town. Dad had promised to take an older kid home who had also been visiting. We knew the kid because he had picked on Joe any number of times in the past, so we were aware that he just generally had an ugly disposition.

As we came out of the house and approached the car, he pushed Joe to the wet ground and shoved his way into the rear seat behind Dad's driver seat. He then exclaimed to Joe and me, "I'm sitting here, punks." Joe began to object, aware of the probable soaking and wanting to caution the kid. He shouted back at Joe and just said, "Shut up, punk." I motioned to Joe to come over and sit with me and then said, "Joe, he's our guest." Joe objected, "But, Ray..." I said again, "guest, Joe, guest."

Dad then raced into the car through the heavy rain from the house, slammed his car door, turned to us momentarily and exclaimed, "Hang on, guys." He hung a left at the corner, headed the three blocks to the always busy Calumet Avenue, then took another left. Calumet Avenue was very wet and very busy, and Dad was in a hurry.

The rest happened very quickly. Dad cut into the outside lane near the curb and gunned it. The rush of water overwhelmed the windshield and the entire car. Then from the other side of the back seat, Joe and I heard this bloodcurdling, intense scream. We looked in the direction of where the kid was sitting, but it was like trying to find him in the middle of Niagara Falls. Eventually his face appeared, but water was dripping from all over him. Joe looked back up at me and tried not to smile. He tried really hard not to smile, but it was hard.

When Joe and I were very young, we were introduced to the world of men and work. My father, Lefty, took us to the nearby country club and told us we could make our own money by working as caddies. Caddying changed us in profound ways. We learned to play a game we would enjoy the rest of our lives. We were introduced to a kind of wealth and a class of people who were, for the most part, powerful and kind. But we were also introduced to a kind of crude, uncivilized behavior for which we had never been prepared. It was for both of us good times and also bad times.

CHAPTER EIGHT

Caddying—a Whole New World

It was a warm, mid-summer day in July of 1950. Joe and I were playing outside in The Weeds. It must have been about 11:00 a.m., for the day was beginning heat up. In the distance, we could hear the jingling of the little bells that announced the little ice cream tricycle truck that came through the neighborhood, block-by-block, with delicious cold delights such as popsicles and ice cream bars. Joe and I knew Dad was home somewhere near the house, so we ran from The Weeds to find him and plead for the nickels that would allow us to purchase our favorite treat— fudge bars.

We found him quickly and made our request. His response that day was both unusual and life-changing. He said, "You need money? Come with me." He walked us to his car and after we got in, he drove us two miles to the country club. Once there, he explained the job of caddying. We listened intently. He then explained that the only way to really understand the job was to see the caddy master, caddy a round of golf making mistakes as every new caddy does, and then apologize to the golfer for the mistakes. That was how we would slowly gain proficiency. Then he left us there.

On that first day Joe got lost on the course, threw his golfer's clubs in the river on the seventh hole and tried to find his way off of the course in order to walk home. On the ninth hole a fellow caddy told me that my little brother was wandering the course, lost and crying. Two other caddies helped me find him just as it was beginning to get dark. When we located him I asked, "Joe, what are you doing?" He responded, "Oh, Ray, thank God it's you. I'm lost in this forest. The guy I was supposed to follow left me with his clubs so I threw them in the river. And I've been trying to find my way out of here ever since." I thanked the caddies I had just met and walked Joe home. He was eight years old.

That first day at the country club was the last day that Joe exhibited such deficiencies. From that point he did nothing but get better. In addition, he quickly developed quite a golf game. We both did. We started with a handful of wooden shafts given to us by our father and two of our uncles. We had a putter; a mid-iron (2), a mashie (5), and a mashie-niblick (7). We also had a wood brassie (2). We had no bag and the golf balls we used were those we found on the course as we caddied. We kept those golf balls in our pockets. In one of our back pockets we always kept our best golf ball—one without smiles—for play on the greens.

Caddies were allowed to play the course every Monday morning and we missed none of these opportunities. We often golfed with several of the Owens or Scartozzi brothers. They were about our age and played the game well. As we improved at our own game, we also improved at the craft of caddying. We eventually got to know every inch of the course, including all of its hazards and idiosyncrasies. We became the caddy master's first choice for visiting golfers in tournament play.

The country club course that we played and caddied had 18 holes—a front nine and back nine. For that time, this course would have been considered a short course, but what the course gave up in distance it made up with its very narrow fairways and thick roughs. From your very first drive on the first hole you had better be in the narrow fairway, or you would find yourself in immediate and significant trouble. In addition, a river of some size ran through the course directly affecting six of the 18 holes. Two additional par three holes had no fairways at all, simply water. Generally speaking, the course was designed to challenge a good golfer. For tournament play, strategic pin locations on the greens could create additional challenges.

For Joe and me and kids like us, the country club and adjoining golf course was like a gigantic garden. It was unlike anything we had ever experienced. The various grasses were always properly cut; the lawns were watered regularly; all bushes and trees were appropriately planted and trimmed; fertilizing and new seeding were applied regularly. The entire course abounded with flowers planted appropriately for the spring, summer and fall seasons. The garden, as we saw it, was constantly being tended to and it provided for us a serene and calm atmosphere—one that we would never forget.

I'll also never forget the caddy Monday we lost our only wood—the brassie. We were on the 11th hole, a par 5 with the river running through it. If you hit a really good drive, you might be able to go over the river with your second shot and be lying right in front of the green. Or, your second shot could go into the river. I was really convinced that I could drive the river with my second shot that day if I hit a great two-wood, so I asked Joe to being me the brassie.

After a couple of practice swings, I let loose, hips and all. I think it was a really great shot, but none of us in the foursome that day will ever know, for the head of the club, after contact with the ball separated from the shaft and flew in a perfect arc directly for the bank of the river. As we all watched, we saw it clear the bank and disappear. A moment later we heard a faint "plunk." I remember just standing there with my mouth open and shaft pointing skyward. I looked around and observed Joe and the other two guys in our foursome. We were all like statues, eyes fixated on the bank. Then in one simultaneous moment we lost it—we were either on our knees, or lying on the ground laughing hysterically. It was not a moment we would ever forget or stop talking about. We never did look for the head of the club; we figured after years with my dad, and uncles, and us, it had earned its resting place.

During the time we were growing up, caddies did not come from affluent families. Caddies were from the poor and working classes. They were the same kids who had paper routes, set pins at the bowling alleys, stocked grocery shelves, and repaired their own bikes if they broke down. They were sometimes scouts, sometimes altar boys, but they could also do things that could and should have gotten the attention of the police.

They could be crude, but they could also be polite, so they could pick up a not fully-smoked cigarette butt from the sidewalk, smoke it, then turn around and give up their seat on a bus to an old lady who couldn't find one. In their life as caddies they never bought a golf ball, never owned a set of clubs. Over the years, they learned from older caddies how to repair their own clubs reasonably well when they broke down. Those who enjoyed the game got fairly good at it. As they found golf balls, they would create their own shag bag with as many as 80 to 100 balls. They would then find a favorite quiet place to practice— one club at a time. For Joe and me it was The Weeds. Those quiet long moments from so long ago continue today to be a precious memory, one club at a time.

Joe was one of the kids who really got good at the game. When you watched him swing a golf club, you saw one single, totally artistic motion. The club and his body became one. He did it with such grace, elegance, and calm. One of his favorite activities was to take a club and simply swing back and forth, back and forth, back and forth. He might swing in that same spot 60, 70, or 80 times without tiring and never losing his graceful calm. He loved the club and it seemed to favor him. At the age of 14, he won his first caddy tournament, and by 17 he had won several more.

When Joe went out to The Weeds to shag, you might not know when he would return. Often times after it finally got dark, mom would ask me to go get him, for his supper had long ago turned cold. I'd go out into the early dark night to find him. Upon approaching his location I might say, "Joe, you're gonna lose all your golf balls out here. It's dark." He might often just look up at me, smile and say, "Let's go pick 'em up, Ray." We would walk about eighty yards or so parallel to the tracks and soon there would be some 70 to 80 golf balls in a fairly tight cluster lying together on the ground precisely where he had aimed. "Oh, Ray," he would say, "There should be a couple of others over there. Could you get 'em for me?" What could I say? He knew that he had missed the center of the cluster with only two balls. I just shook my head, grabbed the two strays, smiled, and helped him fill the bag.

We caddied in those days mostly for men, and over the years we learned what we called the hazards and idiosyncrasies of the "clubbers." They had money, but they also had good manners. They did not flaunt their money, nor did they demean their fellow man. They were fun to caddy for. You could easily like them, and it was clear that they liked you. Then there were those who didn't belong—though they desperately wanted to. They usually had neither money nor manners. They were very often boorish and without character. To paraphrase a line from the movie *A Few Good Men,* "Nobody liked them very much."

With either group, however, you understood that you were of the servant class. You learned this mostly because of the indiscreet way that they spoke in front of you. As a caddy you got to know from their open conversations, who was sleeping with whom, who really had money and power, what their kids were up to, and any number of personal things that you would have assumed would remain private. It was as if we were not there—simply another part of the servant class. They didn't involve us beyond the needs we were expected to take care of. There was a well-understood line regarding our relationship.

One clear exception comes to mind. During a two-day business tournament, one of the younger, new country club members crossed that line, and I was forced to confront him. Joe and I were caddies in the same foursome. Joe was one of the youngest "A" caddies at the country club. Yet, despite his age, he had already become very good at his craft. Our golfers had just finished the 15th green and were now waiting to begin play on the 16th hole. The 16th was a very short water hole. On this tournament day, the sponsors and players had agreed that if a golfer made a hole in one, he would receive a new Cadillac convertible.

To distract the golfers as they hit their tee shots on this hole, someone had hired a voluptuous young lady who would either show her bare breasts as the golfer prepared to swing, or raise her skirt to reveal her lack of under clothing. The fiasco had created a glut of golfers on the 16th tee awaiting their turns. This was about 100 yards from the 15th green where my foursome was waiting along with a dozen caddies from foursomes ahead of us who had not yet had a chance to tee off on the 16th hole.

For some reason that I will never understand, one of the boorish, half-drunk new country clubbers ahead of us on the 16th tee saw my brother Joe who was the smallest of our group of caddies. We were some distance away from him when he shouted at Joe to come to the 16th tee. We older caddies could sense that this guy just wanted to mess with Joe, using him in some way with the young lady. Several of the young golfer's friends on the tee were now also laughing, and motioning for Joe to come to their location on the tee. Joe dropped his golf bag to the ground and began to walk in their direction when I reached out, grabbed

63

him by the collar, and told him to stay where he was. Joe objected saying, "But, Ray, the golfers want me up there."

Then the golfer shouted to me, "Hey, you. Leave him alone. We want him up here." I shouted back, "No." Then he began to leave the tee in a huff and started coming in my direction, shouting obscenities as he came. By this time, everyone in that area was watching. Except for the exchanges the golfer and I were shouting, it was absolutely silent. When he got to within 40 yards of Joe and me, I nervously shouted, "Sir, I've got a bag of golf clubs here and I'm not afraid to use one of them. So if I were you, I would stop right there." I then nervously pulled out a mid-iron and let go of the bag I was holding. He was clearly enraged, but he stopped.

I don't remember much of the rest of that afternoon, except for meetings with the vice-chairman of the county club and the caddy master. I was sure Joe and I would be fired but that never happened. Afterwards, no one else seemed to talk much about it. However, a couple of weeks later on the 18th green as I finished caddying for Mrs. Brenshaw, she stopped me on the way to the clubhouse and asked, "Raymond, you and some other caddies are the ones who created such a row several weeks ago on the 16th tee, aren't you?"

I looked up sheepishly and said, "Yes ma'am."

She then pulled out her little change purse and, while digging in it, said with a smile, "I don't normally do this." She gently handed me a crisp $10.00 bill, turned, and walked into the clubhouse with the other women in her foursome. None of us ever again saw that young county member who had provoked the incident, nor did the country club ever again have that young lady or any other young lady entertaining the guys on the 16th tee or any other tee, for that matter.

Life at the country club slowly went back to normal and routines reestablished themselves. Some days were slower than others, so occasionally the afternoons might drag. In such cases the caddies might pass the time at horseshoes, checkers, and knife games. The most popular knife games were splits and mumblety-peg. Mumblety-peg had so many variations that no one really knew all of the rules. We just knew that in the end the loser had to pull the stick out of the ground with only his teeth.

On really hot days, Joe and I, along with other caddies, would sometimes call it a day after caddying only 18 holes. We had the opportunity to caddy a second round, but if the temperature hovered around 90 or 95 we might just get on our bikes and leave the country club. On those days we often bought a bag of oranges at some fruit stand and then found a shady tree in a forested area where we could rest, look up at the blue sky, and feast on our treat. After a while we might just lie or sit and enjoy some afternoon sun. It was just great to be young, but youth and innocent moments were soon to come to a savage end.

"Blessed are the clean of heart, for they shall see God."

Matthew 5:8

CHAPTER NINE

Looking Into the Eyes of God

The day started out pretty much like most of those mid-August hot days. It was already warm at 7:00 a.m. when Joe and I were on our way to caddy at the country club. His bike was busted, so we were riding double on mine. I was peddling while Joe sat precariously on the front handlebars. It was dangerous. All he would have had to do was allow his foot to drop down and hang too close to the front wheel and spokes and we instantly would have had quite a mess. It worked out, however.

By noon we had finished our first round of caddying, eaten our baloney sandwiches, and started a game of mumblety-peg. We had set up the game under one of the giant trees that separated the caddy area from the trail adjacent to the course which went from the first tee to the tenth.

Right about this time, some 20 yards behind us a large fight was breaking out. We both turned and saw a lot of guys standing in a big group. More guys were running from other areas of the caddy grounds to join them. They were very loud. Near their center there appeared to be some kind of fight. Most of the guys looked older than we were, maybe 16 or 17, and some didn't even look familiar.

Finally, there was a break in the crowd, so Joe and I could see, though not clearly, what was going on. One really big kid had a much smaller kid forced on his knees, pulling the kid's face to his crotch. The big kid's pants were down. The little guy was fighting back, crying and screaming to get away. Then with great force the big kid used his other hand in a clinched fist to hit the kid squarely in the face. Blood from the small kid's face seemed to splash everywhere. He hit the ground with a loud thud. Then several other big kids started to try and kick him as he attempted to escape, crawling as fast as he could on his knees. As he scurried, they continued to kick him, laughing hysterically as they did so. One caught him squarely on the side of the head. I didn't think he'd move after that, but he did.

I looked over at Joe and could see tears streaming down his face. Neither of us had ever in our lives seen such brutality and hostility—nothing even close. I looked back and saw the kid finally break loose. He continued on his knees as some of the bigger guys began throwing some bricks that were lying around on the ground. He was heading in the direction of the tracks some 150 yards away off the country club grounds. He finally got up and was now running, but his attackers continued to throw the bricks. I looked for Joe, but he was gone. Then, out of the corner of my eye, I could see Joe running after the kid.

I screamed out Joe's name, but the noise of the crowd was too loud for him to hear me. I ran. I ran as fast as I could after my little brother whom I believed to be in harm's way. I ran behind him past the soaring bricks. For some reason, no one was following, and soon we neared the tracks. Now it was just the kid, my brother Joe, and me. As the kid approached the tracks, he reached down, grabbed a big stone, turned, and screamed at Joe, "Don't come any closer or I'll throw it." Joe stopped and just stood there for a moment looking at the kid who was shaking— his face and shirt covered in blood. He wasn't very big, kind of skinny really, but he was bigger than Joe who was only ten. Then my brother did something I'll never forget.

He started walking slowly and quietly toward the kid. Somewhat startled, the kid backed up, falling across the first railroad track and screamed again. "I'll throw it. I mean it. I'll throw it." Joe just kept coming slowly. Then Joe stopped and opened his arms wide. A moment passed, and the rock fell from the kid's hand and, as he wept uncontrollably, he fell into Joe's arms.

They were together draped across the track—the kid in Joe's arms. Joe held the boy's bleeding head and face against his chest and then looked at me with a look that I had never before seen. As I looked into my little brother's eyes, I could feel throughout my entire body and soul something pure, and good, all-calming and all-caring. My brother's eyes were, in that moment, not his alone. There was clearly someone with him, and that someone I will always believe was God.

Joe and the sobbing boy stayed there together for a long time. Joe continued to hold him. He held him until the boy slowly let go. When the boy finally left us, he walked down the tracks in a direction we never took. When he got some distance away, he turned, stopped, and waved. We waved back. We never saw him again.

To that time in my life, I had always just accepted on faith that God was real. I didn't after that. I didn't need to. The faith that I had relied on to that point was no longer necessary. I had looked into God's eyes that day and God had looked back.

The Hammond Yellow Jackets was a semi-pro football team that played during the Great Depression of the 1930s. Team membership came from young men of the East Hammond Polish ghetto near Chicago. In the story that follows, team members, though themselves living in poverty and, for the most part destitute, must find a way to help the mother of two of their teammates—Walt and Lefty. They must find a way to help her celebrate with her family "Wigilia," the most important of Polish dinners, taken only on one day a year— Christmas Eve.

The story is titled "The Christmas Purse," and comes in shortened form from the book Yellow Jacket Football in Hard Times and Good.

CHAPTER TEN

The Christmas Purse

During the Great Depression, many poor women did house work for families of means. The homes of the affluent were normally in neighborhoods distant from the homes of the poor. To get to work, a poor woman usually had only two options: take a bus that would cost her five cents each way or walk. The option that was always taken, even in bad weather, was to walk, for that saved her a dime, and a dime was the price of a loaf of bread. The path taken to work by Walter's and Lefty's mother Mary followed along the tracks of the railroad. When she got near her destination, she would leave the tracks to get to the neighborhood and house where she was employed.

House-cleaning work was much sought after. It was clean and in pleasant surroundings. It provided consistent work two to three days per week. Although the pay was only about 15 cents per hour, an average week's pay of roughly $3.00 covered a family's weekly food needs, and sometimes there was enough left over to purchase another much-needed item like a pair of shoes. Most men at that time were unemployed, so the money earned by the mother and, perhaps, her daughters provided the primary and often only source of family income. Young men like Mary's sons, Walter and Lefty, could sometimes find part time work, but those jobs were scarce.

Crisis

It was Friday, December 21, 1934, three days before the Polish Wigilia, the Christmas Eve traditional meal. At 6:15 p.m. the temperature outside was only 18 degrees and it was also very windy. Mary was very late coming home from work. Walt, Lefty, and Pa were getting very nervous. On Fridays, she was normally home by 3:30 p.m. Lefty was getting dressed to go out looking for her.

At that moment, the back door swung open violently and Mary, tripping on the top step, fell hard onto the slippery kitchen floor. She was a short, stout woman, having much the look of hard-working Polish mothers of that day. Lefty and Wolf were quickly by her side. Pa and their younger sister Anne came rushing from the living room a moment later. As the young men lifted her, they could feel that her hands were icy cold and see that both hands were covered in blood. Further, blood was running down the front of both legs from her knees which appeared to be badly scratched, bruised, and dirty. Somewhere she had lost her head scarf and her hair was in a total state of disarray. Her face was beet-red and dirty, while her ears, like her hands, felt frozen.

She looked up, sobbing and breathing heavily. At that moment, Pa gently moved his two sons Walter and Lefty aside, and lifting her into his arms, just looked at her and said quietly and gently, "Mary, Mary." He held her there for a while in the kitchen while she continued to sob, then turned to his eldest son Walt and asked him to make a comfortable place for her in the living room. He then took her there and her daughter Anne tended to her.

When she finally calmed a bit, they asked her what had happened, and she explained that she had lost her change purse on the way home and that it contained this week's wages of $2.70, her Christmas Eve meal money. She said she knew she had it when she was on the tracks because while walking there she had used her handkerchief to wipe her face, and she had felt the change purse in her coat pocket. When she was still on the tracks, but nearer home, she felt for it again, but it was gone. She said from that point she searched and searched, often on her hands and knees, but couldn't find it. It was getting dark so she came home to get a flashlight before continuing her search. She then wept again.

The Search

Lefty, visibly shaken, looked at his mother and said, "Don't worry, Ma, we'll find it." Then to Walt, he said, "Ready?" Walt responded, "Let's get our coats and a flashlight."

As they walked to the tracks, Lefty and Walt stopped at Kal Borbely's house to let him know that they wouldn't be home and that Lefty wouldn't be able to get together later as he and Kal had planned. They also told Kal what they were about. After that Walt and Lefty walked to the tracks. It was still windy and even colder now that it was dark. They started with the location where their Ma told them she first felt the purse gone. Next, very slowly and with their flashlight on, they walked her route all the way to where she would have begun to walk the tracks. They found nothing. It was now near 8:30 p.m. and getting colder. They turned back and began to retrace their steps—a bit less confident.

As they walked, they could see down the tracks several lights in the distance. Moving closer, they could hear voices and saw that the lights though faint seemed to be moving in their direction. Shortly thereafter they heard a shout from a voice they immediately recognized to be Kal Borbely's.

"Hey, what you two guys doin' on the tracks? Tryin' to steal coal?"

Lefty asked, "That you, Kal?"

Kal replied, "Who the hell do you think it is—an early Santa Claus with a bunch of elves?"

By this time Walt and Lefty were coming up on a group of eleven to twelve of their Yellow Jacket football team members. Walt yelled out, "What are all you guys doin' out here?" Johnny Gorski responded, "We heard that the last engineer who came racing through here shook his train and there's enough coal on these tracks for all of East Hammond."

As Johnny approached Walt, he said, "Hi, Walt."

Walt responded, "Thanks for comin', Johnny."

Johnny responded.

"Hey, bunch of us were just sittin' around a warm fire at Wusik's gas station, just gettin' fat and needing a brisk walk outdoors when Kal told us about your Ma losing her change purse. So, what can we do?"

Walt said, "Well, how 'bout if we all stay together, spread out along the track, and slowly walk back and forth for the whole distance that Ma walked until we find it." Gorski agreed, "That's as good a plan as any. Let's do it."

For the next three hours on that cold, windy night, the band of Yellow Jackets searched along the track. Back and forth. Back and forth. Back and forth. It was now nearing midnight when from behind Walt and Lefty who were in the lead along the track, Gorski exclaimed, "We found it." Walt and Lefty turned and raced back to where Gorski and the others were standing. Everyone gathered around Gorski who had both of his hands overlapped and cupped together. He then opened his hands and exposed an overflowing pile of coins, mostly nickels and pennies. The Yellow Jackets gathered around smiling as Lefty and Walt stood dumbstruck. Gorski then said, "It's $2.61. Somehow nine cents fell out of your Ma's purse."

They had given every penny they had.

Walt looked into Johnny's eyes, and shaking his head slowly said, "No, Johnny, we can't take this money from you guys."

Johnny simply said, "We ain't givin' it to you and Lefty. It's for an old lady, sitting in your living room praying to her God with her rosary beads that her sons will find her purse with her Christmas meal money like they promised they would."

Lefty just stood there, his arms limp and down at his side. He was overwhelmed. As he raised his head, the tears streaming down his face made it clear that he was having trouble holding it all together. He took a deep breath, swallowed hard and, shaking his head, just looked into the eyes of his friends, this band of Yellow Jackets.

At close to 1:00 a.m. that morning, Ma got her $2.61. She knew it wasn't hers because she had two dollar bills, two quarters, and two dimes in her change purse. But they made her take it. She was never told who specifically was out there that night, but from that day, whenever some Yellow Jackets were in the house, there was always a small pot of coffee brewing on the stove.

The little change purse was never found.

Friends

I think that there will never be,

A friend as dear as you to me;

A friend of whom I'm always sure,

Whose faith and loyalty endure,

..

Who magnifies the good in me

Yet overlooks the faults there be;

Good friends are often found 'tis true,

But **God** *sends a friend like you.*

Sonia Aquino Asuncion-Bennie

The lines quoted above are from a poem given to Ray by a dear friend and fellow seminarian, Jimmy O'Connor

The following Story of God's gift of friends is taken in modified form from the book, *Sweet Land of Liberty.* It is included to emphasize God's gift of a friend to offer support, compassion, and love.

CHAPTER ELEVEN

Friends

"Ray, where we goin'?" "I told you, Joe, on a raft in a river. But stop talkin' about it or Busia will be askin' a lot of questions."

"Okay, Ray."

"Rajmund, you beh get egg from coop."

"Okay, Busia. I'm goin.'"

I ran out to the chicken coop and got five eggs for our breakfast.

As we were finishing eating, there was a knock on the back side door. Busia from the back porch exclaimed, "Rajmund, Bobby eh Stefan beh here." Then she said to the boys, "You beh come in."

Bobby said to Busia, "Thanks, Busia. Want a fresh doughnut from the O.K. Bakery?" Busia beamed. Bobby knew that the O.K. Bakery doughnut was her soft-spot. I gave Bobby a dirty look.

"What? *What?!!*"

"You know what."

Then Bobby asked, "Rajmund, you gotta bag?"

I found one and shoved it in his chest while Busia poured her hot coffee to drink with what she didn't understand was her stolen doughnut.

Bobby then said to Joe, "Hey, kid, you comin' with us?"

Joe, finishing up his eggs, just smiled and nodded. Then Stefan reminded Joe,

"Don't forget the new slingshot we made for you."

Joe pointed to his left rear pocket. Then Busia questioned, "Where you going?"

"Just bummin' around, Busia. Don't worry."

Five minutes later we were out the door, the four of us, each with a slingshot hanging out of a back pocket and Bobby with a fairly sizable bag of booty.

"O.K., Bobby, so what did you get?"

"Ten, Rajmund, ten, a new record. Well, now nine, figuring the one I gave to Busia."

I interjected, "I told you before, you can't give Busia stolen shit."

"O.K. O.K. Next time I'll pay for hers. Still feel sticky—had 'em all under my shirt. Looked like Stefan when I came out of the bakery."

Stefan objected angrily,

"I ain't fat, Bobby. I'm big-boned. My Ma told me so."

"Well, then, you got the bones of a rhino."

"Gonna kick your ass right here, Bobby."

I jumped in and separated them and then said, "C'mon, guys. C'mon. It's a bright sunny day and we're on our way to have fun on the river. So, let's not ruin it with another fight."

Bobby was a favorite of my dad Lefty. Maybe he felt this way because Bobby didn't have a pa, maybe because of his forever bright smile, or maybe simply because Bobby was East Hammond through and through. Whatever it was, Lefty liked him and so did Joe and I.

The River

Soon we had left the familiarity of our neighborhood and had begun the one mile walk to the Little Calumet River. Bobby eventually parted with four of the doughnuts, including the one for himself. So, the talk and camaraderie became pleasant and would have remained so all the way to the river had Bobby not told Stefan that the doughnut he gave to him came from under his armpit. Nonetheless, we made it and stood just east of Calumet Avenue on the bank of the river.

There wasn't much around that area—a few stores and a gas station, but virtually no homes. Further south on Calumet Avenue, was Ridge Road, the ancient shore of Lake Michigan. But we weren't going that way. Today was a river trip. A couple of months earlier Bobby and I had found an old raft that probably had drifted this way from somewhere near Chicago. It was kind of beat up. So, we had made several trips with leftover tar we borrowed from East Hammond backyard sheds.

The last time here, we had tested the raft and we found it to be reasonably seaworthy. With us on this trip, besides Bobby's stolen doughnuts, were six potatoes and matches. If we could get a good fire going later, the potatoes would only take about an hour. Nothin' like a hot potato out of a fire on a stick. Nothin' like it. Kid brother Joe seemed really excited. This was his first venture out with the guys. Bobby liked Joe a lot. So, Joe being two years younger was never a problem.

"Hey, Ray, Bobby, is this it?" Joe had found the raft.

"Good goin,' Joe."

"Stefan, help Joe get that brush off the raft and let's get under way."

Within ten minutes we were ready to head to the center of the river. We were a little apprehensive because we had never done it with four guys. In addition, the last couple of weeks there had been a lot of rain, so the river was deeper than normal. Even with the heavier load the raft was holding up well, but despite its apparent seaworthy quality and our confidence, we had decided to take off our shoes, roll up our pants legs and go bare-footed.

With the two long, sturdy poles that Bobby and I had made a month ago, we pushed off. Once in the river, it didn't take us long to figure out that this raft ride was gonna be a one-way trip. The river current wasn't treacherous, but it was unquestionably strong. The two poles we had wouldn't be enough to go back up stream. Wherever we decided to leave the raft, we'd have to come back for it another day when the river current was not so strong.

"Rajmund."

"Yeah, Bobby."

"Big bend comin' in the river, and if you haven't noticed, we're goin' faster."

"Everybody hang on."

Up ahead the river appeared to have rapids, and it must have been making a sharp turn because in the distance it looked like it dead-ended and just disappeared. Then we got to the bend and the rapids. But the momentum had us going right toward some big rocks instead of turning with the river. Then we hit. Joe got loose from my arm and Bobby grabbed him. Stefan's pole cracked like a twig, and he nearly got pitched overboard. Then the raft turned and began to head more slowly downstream. It had happened so quickly that we hadn't had time to get scared.

I looked down at Joe under Bobby's arm, then at Bobby. All of a sudden Stefan jumped up and screamed, "The doughnuts!" A moment later we all started laughing—then roaring. We had been more scared than we realized and somehow Stefan's scream about losing the remaining doughnuts seemed hilarious. We had just shot our first rapids on a great river. We still had one pole, a bag of potatoes, and we were alive. Nothin' gets better than that when you're ten. Nothin'.

Soon, we started to sing. Joe started us off. It was from a movie we all knew and the moment couldn't have been more appropriate to the song, *"Zip-a-dee-doo-dah, zip-a-dee-ay, my oh my, what a wonderful day, plenty of sunshine comin' my way, zip-a-dee-doo-dah, zip-a-dee-ay.* We just sang, and sang, and sang all the way down that river. All the way till the river forked.

"All right, guys. This is our stop."

"Rajmund's right, Bobby chimed in. Get ready to jump."

Stefan added, "I'll try to push us to the shore with the pole."

What happened next wasn't quite great seamanship, but we all managed to jump and not get totally soaked. We were now on land and moving south alongside of this large tributary that fed into the Little Calumet. We all noticed that its current was actually swifter than the larger river we had just left.

Stefan shouted out, "Rajmund, where we headed?"

"To the dam up ahead. Bobby and I were here 'bout a month ago."

Then Bobby interjected, "Let's find a place to cook the potatoes somewhere around here in these deep woods so they'll be ready for us on the way back."

"Good idea."

Bobby took the lead. Then he looked back for us and as he did, he tripped over one of the many half-buried fallen trees and fell flat on his face in the mud and leaves. As we rushed to see if he was hurt and gathered around him, he looked up, spit out some leaves, got to his knees and shouted a Polish curse, "Pshaw-clef, oletta."

Joe's eyes got very wide and big. Then Bobby looked directly at Joe and said, "Don't ever say that. It's not very nice." Joe smiled.

Stefan added, "You been hangin' around your dziadzia (grandfather) too much, Bobby."

We finally got to a good spot. Then we dug a hole nice and deep, filled it with some dry, bigger, slow-burning logs, and then added our six potatoes right in the middle. We covered the whole thing with some kindling and some smaller logs and cleared away all the dry brush from around the area. Within ten minutes we had a roaring fire. We waited about ten more minutes for the fire to calm down. When it did, we threw on some more twigs and several big logs for good measure. We all felt that we had done a pretty good job. So, now we were on our way back to the river and the dam. We figured the dam to be about a half-mile walk, at most, and before we got there, we would be able to hear the water coming over the dam.

A Lasting Shared Vision

It didn't seem to take any time at all for the woods to thin of the massive trees and for more and more light to come rushing though from above, touching larger and larger patches of ground and lower branches of the younger trees. We were leaving the forest. The distant light was even brighter and the faint sound that we couldn't initially identify we now knew was the sound of rushing water. And then there it was—the dam.

There is hardly a memory so deep and pure as the memory of coming through a pristine forest on a summer afternoon with friends, also age 10, whose senses, like yours, are virgin to the experience that awaits. I don't remember stopping, though we must have. I just remember Joe saying, "Wow!" Bobby and I looked down at him standing between us, then recognized that we were all motionless, just standing in awe. For us, it might as well have been the Niagara Falls, and it was now ours. We had travelled the mighty river, trekked through the primeval forest and together had found the great fall of water racing over the dam into a magnificent pool below.

A primitive, collective yell went up from all of us, and within minutes we were splashing in the waters beneath the dam wearing nothing more than our birthday suits. We splashed, dove in and out, cannon-balled where we could, horse-played, splashed some more, held our breath under water, and eventually sat or lay together on the shore, and soaked up the good sun. No one spoke. Time just drifted by as we simply lay still and enjoyed the moment.

Then..."Hey, Bobby."

"Yeah, Joe."

"Look at these little round rocks around the edge of the water. They're like marbles."

Bobby excitedly exclaimed, "Rajmund, Stefan, look. Little Joe's right. They're absolutely perfect for ammunition for our sling shots and there's hundreds of 'em, maybe thousands."

We dressed within a flash and then carefully collected and loaded our pockets. It's not often you find a perfect rock for your slingshot and here Joe had found hundreds of them. As we sifted through the sand, it was almost impossible to find bad ones, except maybe a few that were too big. All the way back to our potatoes in the deeper woods we fired randomly. We fired at tree trunks in the distance. We fired at leaves, branches, and occasional birds, though with all the noise we were making the birds seemed to know to keep their distance.

Finally, we arrived at our fire and the potatoes, and our timing couldn't have been better. Bobby, Stefan, and I sharpened some sticks with our knives. We uncovered the potatoes. As we pierced their skins with our sticks, it was clear that they were ready and so were we. We took all of them out and then waited a bit for them to cool enough to bite into.

"Hey, Bobby."

"Yeah, Rajmund."

"Stefan says you have a birthday comin' up."

"Yeah...be eleven in about a week."

"Eleven? Bullshit. You're gonna be ten, like me."

"Gonna be eleven. Got held back in first grade. Stefan's already eleven. Got held back too. You're the only smart one, Rajmund."

I didn't say anything. Just sat there eating my potato. Never knew that about Bobby and Stefan. Some things you just never get told about, I guess.

The potatoes were about the best we had ever eaten, probably because we were so hungry. Then we walked back to that place near the Calumet River where we had left our shoes. On the way we shot at every tree, every telephone pole. We even shot at some carp in the river. Didn't get any, though. Once we got our shoes on, we walked over to Calumet Avenue and began heading back to our neighborhood. Joe started singing "Zip-a-Dee-Doo-Dah," again, so we all joined in. It was great. We sang for several blocks, even making up words when we couldn't remember some. We were havin' a ball.

A Full Dose of Hate

Then, right about the time we got to 169th Street, Bobby stopped in front of this little corner grocery store. "Guys, we're gonna have a treat. See, I been holdin' out on ya." Then he reached into his right front pocket past all of the remaining little rocks and pulled out a dime. He then held it up for us to see.

"Little Joe, how many Hostess cupcakes in a package?"

Joe quickly responded, "two."

"And how much for a package of cupcakes, Joe?"

"A nickel."

"Right again. And I have a dime. So we can buy how many, Joe?"

Joe hesitated, but Stefan and I shouted out, "four."

Then Bobby responded, "Treat time—let's go."

The three of us followed Bobby into the store where there were already several adult customers and a clerk who was up front behind the counter. No sooner had we entered the store than the clerk, a fairly big, husky man, shouted to us, "You little kids get the hell outta here."

Bobby responded, "but we're here to buy some cupcakes."

"You didn't hear what I said?"

"Why you bein' so mean, mister?"

"You little shits live down there?" as he pointed north toward East Hammond.

"Yeah," replied Bobby.

He came very quickly out from behind his counter with a long axe handle, and as he came toward us he yelled, "Get your Polish asses outta here. I don't want you little Polack sons-of-bitches in here, and I don't have to sell to you."

We were all backing out as quickly as we could for he had the long axe handle raised over his head. Bobby was peddling backwards and tripped over Stefan and then went down in the doorway. The little rocks from his pockets went everywhere and his slingshot fell at his feet. By this time, the man had reached Bobby and, seeing the slingshot, smashed it with the end of his axe handle while I grabbed Bobby under his arms and pulled him onto the sidewalk outside of the store. The man then stood in the doorway and yelled, "Now get your little Polack asses back to your own neighborhood before I call the police."

As we ran, we yelled some vulgarities and profanities, but we knew even as we did that it did no good. Within a few minutes, we got to Columbia Avenue, turned left and kept running all the way to the city incinerator and massive water tower. We were back in the neighborhood. We hadn't said much. We had been running most of the way. When we got to Stefan's house, he went his way and from his doorstep simply turned and waved goodbye.

It's What Friends Do

Next stop was Bobby's on Kenwood Street. When we got there, now walking, Joe grabbed Bobby's sleeve and tugged on it several times. Bobby looked down and Joe said, "Our Busia has lots of kapusta to eat, so you have to come to our house."

Bobby looked down at Joe and gave him a kind of affectionate laugh, and so did I. Then I said, "Tell your Ma you gotta stay with us tonight."

Bobby looked at me, then down again at Joe who was smiling. He nodded and went and told his Ma.

When we walked into Busia's back side door, she came out from the kitchen, looked down at the three of us, smiled, chuckled, shook her head and said, "Yeh beh clean first, then yeh eat, but yeh not eat till you beh clean. And don't beh make mess in the bathroom!"

Three forest and river warriors hit the tub all at once and after some vicious scrubbing and drying, we were sitting at a kitchen table much hungrier than we thought we were. Busia's bright smile and warm kapusta and buttered rye bread were pushing back an ugly experience and unanticipated pain. More than anything, Bobby and I, though we did not speak of it that day, were most upset with ourselves for not seeing it coming. Such ugliness directed at us had not been the first time, nor did we expect it to be our last.

Like our parents before us, we had grown up in the safety of our Polish neighborhood where we were known and could, therefore, completely relax in our personal uniqueness and community ethnicity. We had also, over the years, come to understand that this kind of safety and security ended at the neighborhood boundaries. The world could be a beautiful place and it could equally be brutal and evil.

The deepest hurt and pain that we felt that day was the pain we felt for Joe. He had not really seen this kind of hateful prejudice before and we did not want this for him. He loved us both so much and we felt the pain of having let him down. He had now seen first-hand a part of the darker side of God's creation.

That night after supper, Busia let us lie on the floor in the living room and listen to some of our favorite radio programs. On this particular night first was "Captain Midnight." Then a real treat in the form of "The Lone Ranger." And finally "Straight Arrow." Halfway through "Straight Arrow" Joe fell asleep. Aunt Rose gave us her bed in the front bedroom that night. She sometimes did that when it was two or three of us and, therefore, a bit too tight for the single bed in the middle bedroom. Bobby and I put Joe in the middle so there'd be no worry about his falling out or being kicked out during the night.

93

As we all lay there starting to doze off, Joe half asleep said, "Ray was that real mad guy in the store talkin' about me too?"

Before I had a chance to respond, Bobby said, "No, little Joe, he wasn't talkin' about you. He was just talkin' about us big guys. Right, Rajmund?"

"Right, Bobby."

"Now you just go to sleep and don't worry about that stuff, Joe."

Joe quietly responded, "Okay."

After a while, I looked over at Bobby and in the dim moonlight saw a tear slowly work its way down the side of his nose. He glanced up at me, saw me looking at him then brushed it aside and said, "Got somethin' in my eye." He then turned over. Shortly thereafter, I did too.

Joe and I had an older brother who died before we ever got to know him. As I drifted off to sleep that night, I remember thinkin' that Bobby would have been a good older brother. Maybe God in his way was trying to make up for our loss. Maybe that's how God spends most of his free time—making up for such losses. Putting a friend back where one was taken away. From what I can tell, it must keep Him pretty busy.

Bobby Goes Home

Many years later as I was sitting in my office, I got a call from a close friend, Captain Diego, a narcotics officer in Chicago. Diego's relationship with Bobby went way back and Bobby's early influence had resulted in Diego going into law enforcement instead of a life of street crime. The message was short and simple. Bobby had died in prison. I hung up the phone, sat for a moment, and then called Joe.

Years ago Bobby had said to Joe and me that if God took him first to send up a prayer. Said he felt he would need it. Said he wanted it from guys that God would recognize as his close friends. He thought that might get God's attention since God had been the one who had made us friends in the first place. Then he made us promise. On the phone Joe wept and then told me he would pick up dad and meet me at Saint Mary's Church in the old neighborhood.

On my way to the church I pulled off to the side of the road near Conkey and Fields Streets. I stopped and turned my lights off. I lowered my car window and looked out to the other side of the street. It looked as it did many years ago. Almost nothing had changed except for the absence of Bobby and me, two little street kids who used to fight there. The snow was coming in and I was getting wet. But I just sat there staring. Through the falling snow I could almost see them, couldn't tell who was winning, but then that never really mattered to us, just as long as it was a fair fight.

I turned my lights back on and began to drive. It was only now a couple of blocks to St. Mary's Church. Joe's car was already there with maybe a half-hour of fresh snow melting on it. I parked and walked to the church. Joe had obviously gotten someone to open up. I opened the heavy church door. It was kind of a quiet dark inside.

The red sanctuary lamp was lit and hanging high above the tabernacle, and there were a number of candles burning and creating a warm glow in front of the Blessed Virgin's altar. My eyes adapted quickly as I walked toward the communion rail and main altar. I could see two figures sitting in the front pew, now turned and looking toward me.

"Hi, Pa...Joe. Thanks for bein' here."

Then Lefty looked at me and just asked, "Polish or English, Kid?"

"I think he'd like Polish, Pa.....I'm sure he would."

He nodded, waited for me to kneel with them, and then with the Sign of the Cross we began, "Wimie Ojca i Syna i Ducha...."

Three Polish East Hammond street kids were answering the request of a friend—another Polish street kid who had "gone home." As we prayed that early evening, I'm sure in the background quiet of that old church I could hear the sound that the saw makes with the file when they are in harmony.

'There are more things in heaven and earth, Horatio, then are dreamt of in your philosophy."

Hamlet

CHAPTER TWELVE

From a Hilltop

Most 20-year-olds don't really have a clue as to what they want to do with their lives. I was certainly part of that group. I had graduated high school, had worked laboring jobs in various mills such as Inland Steel, Standard Forge, and JT Steel Corporation. I had studied engineering at Purdue and accounting and social work at St. Josephs College in East Chicago. I volunteered to instruct young altar boys in the Latin liturgy of the Mass, and I also taught religion classes for high school students in the evenings. Success came easy—satisfaction not so much.

Unanticipated by me, however, a life-direction change was preparing to whack me on the side of the head. I believe it started at 5:30 a.m. Mass. That morning, I was the altar server for Father Larry Heeg. As was the case with such early Masses, it was sparsely attended. He and I came out of the sacristy appropriately robed and then stood next to each other at the foot of the altar—a position very familiar to me as I was often there teaching the novice altar boys.

I began the Mass with the sign of the cross in Latin, "In nomine Patris, et Filii, et Spiritus Sancti. Amen. Then I continued, "Introibo ad altare Dei."

Father Heeg responded, "Ad Deum qui laetificat juventutem meam."

On and on, prayer after prayer, we continued with the opening prayers for this very early morning Mass—both of us not yet quite awake. We got all the way to the first long prayer—the Confiteor. He stopped, stood motionless for a long moment, and then looked down at me and whispered, "Ray, Ray, you're saying my part."

It dawned on me—he's right. So I whispered back. "What do you want to do...should we keep going?"

He responded, "We can't do that. I've got to do my own part. I'm the priest."

We both began to laugh quietly. Finally, I said, "It would be quicker if we just keep going."

"Ray, I'm the priest. Take it from the top."

After Mass, we changed back into our street clothes and straightened out the sacristy. I had something on my mind, but there would be time later to talk about it. Later that day we were going to do some water skiing on Cedar Lake. I was sure we would be able to talk then.

The mid-afternoon was beautiful. Father Heeg had finished his priestly duties and we were getting his boat, a gift from his family, out of the garage of a friend from the parish. The trip to

Cedar Lake was quick and the water skiing excellent. The lake was like a sheet of glass and we had taken full advantage. We were now anchored in a quiet cove. The time seemed right, so I asked, "Father, do you think I would fit in the seminary?"

He looked up and then said with a smile.

"Well, Ray, if you do decide to go, you do have an edge. You can already say Mass like a priest."

I smiled and nodded my head.

Vision Quest

A couple of months later with the Bishop's approval I was on my way to Saint Lawrence Seminary in Mount Calvary, Wisconsin. This seminary was run by the Capuchin Franciscans who had established the school in 1860. The school had a long history of educating diocesan priests. Among them was the very honored and respected Bishop Noll who began his study for the priesthood there in 1888. The only request I made of my bishop when he was picking a seminary for me was that he please select a school that was not too affluent or comfortable. After arriving at Saint Lawrence, a seminary built on a hill in Wisconsin, I concluded that he had carefully kept my request in mind.

By 1960, providing students with semi-private rooms with a bath was a fairly standard practice in colleges and seminaries across the country. However, the facilities at Saint Lawrence were much sparser. Students were housed in old military-style dorms with community baths. The classrooms were very old and drafty with strong winds coming through the walls in winter months. There was a pool, but it was several hundred yards down the hill, a significant distance from other facilities. But, after heavy rains, swimming was a bit of a challenge since clay holes do tend to collect a lot of water and the sides of this kind of pool become very slippery. If a touch of class or up-to-date amenities were what you were looking for in a seminary, Saint Lawrence was, for you, a wrong turn taken. It was in clerical circles referred to as "The Poor Boy's Seminary."

I had attended a seminar for two years when I was old enough to enter high school. Those two years were some of the best of my life. I experienced a classical prep school education, became acquainted with the demands of the life of a priest, made life-long friends, and had a great time. So I thought I was prepared for the kind of life I was going to be engaged in.

But, as a college-aged young man, I became immersed in a life which required a much more sophisticated understanding of academics and humanities. The entire curriculum was much more rigorous. Religious studies included debates and discussions regarding issues in theology and philosophy which, until then, I had not deeply explored. In addition, my fellow students came from a variety of backgrounds. Some of them were older than I, and some had even served in wartime Korea.

But despite the seriousness of our intentions to become priests, I was surprised at the opportunities to enjoy the simple pleasures this life had to offer. And I was surprised at how deeply I was affected by the opportunities to ponder my relationship with God. From days filled with studies, games, and entertainment and with hours filled with quiet, intense reflection, I began to understand that although this place was filled by people like me who had noble goals, we were, in the final analysis, just people searching for answers and would, like everyone else, struggle with our own character flaws and inadequacies.

Ultimately, I would decide to leave and continue to find my path to a different life's work. But the experiences I was privileged to have while at this special place shaped my life in untold ways, and to this day, I carry the memories of those experiences and the people I came to know. So, I am pleased now to share how this time in my life delighted, enriched, and inspired me.

Happy Days

A special delight on days after heavy rains was the river. The river ran through the grounds near the clay swimming hole. If you walked another fifty yards or so beyond the swimming hole, you would come to this river. If there had been no heavy rain, you could walk across by stepping on the rocks, but if you slipped off a rock, you might be knee-deep in water. After a good rain, however, the river became somewhat dangerous. It was much deeper—four feet or so in the middle—and the current became much swifter.

Hanging over the center of the river, a heavy duty rope hung from a secure branch some 25 feet above the river. This was a rope I and my classmates had fashioned so we could swing across, not a very difficult feat when the flow was normal. After a heavy rain that was a different story.

The attempted river-crossing that I still remember most vividly took place in late October. There were five of us jaunting across the damp lowlands that afternoon. Mickey, a classmate, was new to our group, and he often boasted of having acquired a strong background in the science of physics prior to coming to the seminary. We had no sooner gotten to the swollen river when Mickey assessed the situation and declared that he knew a way, based upon the laws of physics, to thrust ourselves from the near bank to the far bank using the hanging rope. I remember that we were all somewhat apprehensive, standing there on the near bank and looking at the rather deep and rapidly moving water.

But Mickey was insistent and confident. He said that he would back far away from the river holding the end of the rope loosely in his right hand and then he would run rapidly to the river's edge and jump. He advised that his momentum would thrust him to the far shore as he clung to the rope. It didn't sound right to any of us, but then none of us had majored in physics. So what would we know?

To this day, I can still picture Mickey's rocking motion before the run—back and forth, back and forth, so rhythmic—then a slight acrobatic jump followed by a run which culminated in a leap high into the air while holding the end of the rope in his right hand. It looked truly magnificent, but paled in comparison to the massive splash that his entire body created as it forcefully met the center of the river.

We all stood near the bank speechless as we watched him slowly sink into the middle of the river, holding onto the rope while desperately attempting to climb out of the water. He finally sunk to shoulder-depth and when he was able to look in our direction, he could see that we were either on our knees, or simply rolling on the ground laughing so intensely we were not able to stand or breathe. After a few long minutes, Mickey himself began laughing and couldn't stop. Eventually, through his laughter he simply yelled out to us on the shore, "So much for Physics." At that point we all got to our feet and jumped in with him.

Folklore?

My earliest academic loves as a child were science and mathematics. I'm not sure why. I do remember my early fascination with the night sky and stars, and later, when I could understand, I remember being captivated by the notion of a solar system. When I was 13, my mother gave me for my Christmas gift a book titled, "Stars." It was produced in color, and I read it over and over again. I couldn't seem to get enough, and my young mind created and recreated speculations of what was "really" out there. Then about the same time, I accidently fell into books of science fiction. What a find. Now, not only could I speculate, but I could read about the speculations of others. And, as I read their speculations, they provoked even more of my own. I found the world of such thinking to be enjoyable and captivating.

My other early love grew out of the studies of my religion. The notion of a creation from nothing, of God's separating night from day, of a great flood covering the entire world, of walking on water, of raising people from the dead, of a second-coming, of the existence of angels, of eternity, miracles, and mystical experiences all fascinated me. But, unlike many of my friends who accepted the stories as absolute truth, the stories prompted me to ask questions about other possibilities. I wondered, for example, if God maybe made another universe where people did not sin. I asked if miracles were much more common than we were lead to believe or if, perhaps, there could be thousands and thousands of saints, not just the few as designated by the Church. I pondered more deeply the possibility of miracles, heavenly visions, and contacts with souls who had long ago passed away.

As my science and mathematics questioning led me to science fiction, my religious questioning and speculation led me to a love of religious folklore. I found myself drawn to it. Again, as with science fiction, I took great pleasure in the religious speculations of others. Eventually, I found there was no better place to hear these kinds of speculations than in the seminary where many others were of the same mind and were willing to share stories and ideas which challenged what most people accept as reality.

I have come to believe that one of God's subtle nudging techniques is to provoke our desire to explore the realms of science fiction and the legends of folklore. God has given us a unique and wonderful way to contemplate, speculate, reflect, or possibly even meditate on profound concepts. Following are two such stories I was told while at the seminary I hope that they do for you what they did for me—give you a bit of a nudge.

A Simple Brother

There was a simple brother who was accepted conditionally into the Capuchin order around 1870. He was a gentle man who was extremely awkward and clumsy. Eventually, because of his limitations, he was warned that if he did not improve, he would be dismissed from the order. Several days after that warning, as he was bringing much-needed water up the hill, he fell and cracked the two wooden buckets which he had filled. He left the buckets and ran to the rector to shamefully and tearfully share what he had done.

Two friars returned with him to find the buckets. But before they went down the hill, they found two wooden buckets filled with water at the top of the hill near the shrine to the Blessed Virgin. The buckets were identical to the buckets always used for this task. The brother could not explain. The friars then accompanied him down the hill to where he said he had fallen. There they found the broken wooden buckets. No one could ever explain where the buckets at the shrine came from.

I so love this story. I really don't care whether or not it is true. I love the story because, for me, it prompts profound questions: Why a miracle for this simple brother? Did he possess the innocence that Christ was speaking of when He said, "Unless you become as little children, you will not enter the kingdom of Heaven." Was it his soul's simplicity that so pleased God? Is this God's preferred direction? It is such a soft nudge, but such a powerful one.

An Uneasy Resting Place

Adjacent to the south wall of the large monastery on the seminary grounds is an area set aside for the cemetery resting place of Capuchin friars. It has been their sacred resting place since 1860. However, something disturbing began happening in the mid-1930s. Priests residing in the monastery began hearing what sounded like knocking. In early evenings, the sound resonated throughout the entire monastery. The friars studied the condition and determined that the knocking sound was coming from the south wall, adjacent to the cemetery. The knocking, which went on for several weeks, continued to grow louder until Masses for the deceased friars began to be offered. When this occurred, the knocking stopped and never started again.

Variations of these kinds of stories or myths seem to be particularly connected to those places we feel are especially holy and sacred. Are they true? I don't know. Many of those who tell them seem to think so.

In the case of the knocking, what is the distance from the living to the dead? Who of us knows? We assume a vast, immeasurable cavern. Are we correct? Is it possible that we are really quite close? Can we allow ourselves to believe that the sacred presence of God or saints might cross over into our world, enhance humanity in a special way, and make us a little holier—if for only for a little while?

A Vision of Harmony

On the seminary grounds there was a baseball field high on the hill. It was so high that if you hit a home run over center field, the ball was pretty much gone as the drop-off was significant. The games played there on pleasant summer and autumn days were always just plain fun. The young bearded priests in their street clothes enjoyed playing, and the brothers, seminary groundskeepers, and cafeteria staff who watched them added to the festive atmosphere. This kind of interaction of shepherds, shepherds-in-waiting, along with a smattering of sheep was so simple and yet so profound.

But it was mid-December now and quite cold. I stood by myself on the highest point of the hill above the baseball field. The games played in the summer and the fall were now over. The several inches of newly-fallen snow crunched beneath my feet, and as I looked out beyond the field into the winter of Wisconsin, I could see forever. The sun was beginning to set and the distant sky was filling with magnificent streaks of oranges, capped by blues and finally blacks. I'm sure there have been prettier skies, but I haven't seen many.

It was the last day of a spiritual retreat. For me it was a good retreat. I am sure the formal structure helped with that—the total silence, the extended time for reflection, the ancient Gregorian chants, the denial of food, the long periods of being alone. Yes, it had been a good retreat, and I stood there watching from that highest point the sun doing its evening magic. As I remember, I didn't have any particular sense of joy or happiness, but rather just had a sense of peace and inner harmony. It was quiet for me both inside and outside.

*Then it happened. I continued to be by myself but felt no longer alone. I felt as though my entire body, soul, and mind were being held—ever so gently. My gaze remained fixated on the setting sun, but then throughout my total and complete cognitive and emotional being **I no longer had any questions. I simply understood**. There was total and complete cognitive clarity of the* *entire universe. Everything was so very simple and interrelated. Harmony was in every piece of everything I had ever known and all I had never known. All was part of a whole. It was as if the veil I had unknowingly been wearing all of my life had been momentarily lifted. I could see for the first time, and all was in harmony and all was good. I had no answers for there were no questions. All was simply understood to be part of the whole. Yet there were no parts, simply the understood whole.*

And then it was over, as suddenly and unexpectedly as it had began. If I suggest that this momentary clarity had lasted a second of time that would be an extreme exaggeration. Its duration was so much less than that. Yet, for me, it was as if forever. I have never been taught to measure anything other than in units of time and, therefore, there is no way to express my understanding of its duration.

For many years after this experience, I questioned my worthiness to have received it. Finally, that became clear. What I had received was a gift, and somehow, for a reason I shall probably never know, God enjoyed giving it. Did I earn it? As I said, it was a gift. Gifts are gifts. They are not wages paid. They are not owed. I know this clearly now, but still I can't get over wanting to someday give something back to God—not tit for tat, not I owe you one, not it's my turn, but rather just a gift. The way it was given to me—simply because I'd enjoy doing it.

Did I see the face of God that day? I don't think so. I think he just wanted to show me what he had made and have me, in that instant, sense the treasure of understanding how everything all fits together. I believe in that instant I got a look at the "Big Star Book."

I think some day He'll show it to me again. I hope so. I think He has shown it to others, and I don't believe that such of His giving is infrequent. I think some day He will show it to all of us. I believe it's partially why He created us. I think He just gets a kick out of sharing things.

So I believe.

As a young man I was overwhelmed by the sudden death of a college classmate whom I very much admired and cared for. His death shook me to the core, but ultimately it was his way of living that helped me find my own purpose. Eventually, I moved on, married, and began to have children. Though I had come to learn that the death of anyone you love is never easily accepted, I had never considered that I might have to face the possibility that one of my children would die at a young age. Thus, the protracted and grave illness of our daughter Tanya at the age of four was a terrifying experience. Her recovery, though long and complicated, gave me and my wife indescribable joy.

I cannot think of anything more heart-wrenching and crushing for anyone than the loss of a child through illness or an accident. Nor can I think of a joy so deep as the joy one sees in the eyes and smile of a child whose life was spared. To look into the face of a child so spared is akin to looking into the face of God.

CHAPTER THIRTEEN

Miracles and a Child's Smile

We named our first child Tanya. She was everything that parents hope for when they discover that God will be giving them the extraordinary gift of a child. Before she could walk, she needed to have casts put on both legs to straighten out severely crooked feet, a condition that at one time was not correctable. Once the casts were on and she began to crawl, she would use her arms to pull herself along so that she could cruise the hardwood floors of our house. It was amazing to watch her jet through hallways, take quick corners, rebound off a dining room wall and then sit up, clap her hands, and scream with delight. She filled our lives with laughter and joy.

Over the next two years, Tanya was joined by her brothers, Michael and Scott. When she was about four years old, we gathered them all together in our car and started out on a vacation. Tanya had not been feeling well that spring, so we had consulted a number of specialists to see what was causing her generalized illnesses and frequent headaches. The issue of headaches was especially worrying, as two children in Marion's family had died from brain tumors. However, after neurological examinations including an EEG, we were assured that there was nothing serious to worry about, so we set out as planned.

We visited relatives and went all the way to New England to show the children the ocean. During this time, Tanya continued to have headaches. We thought she must be having sinus problems or some kind of allergy upsets, as we had been assured she was okay. We stopped at Marion's mother's house in Conneaut, Ohio before making the last leg of our trip back to Indiana. While there, Marion noticed that when Tanya was sleeping, her eyes weren't closing all the way.

Worried, we quickly returned home and called our pediatrician. By the time we got to his office, the right side of Tanya's face was paralyzed. When he saw her condition, he immediately made arrangements for us to take her to Children's Memorial Hospital in Chicago. After we arrived, Tanya was taken very quickly to the neurology unit for an evaluation. Almost immediately she was taken to surgery where Dr. Raimondi placed a shunt into her brain to relieve the pressure that the tumor had caused by blocking the flow of spinal fluid. As we sat together in the waiting room that night, I looked at Marion. I knew she was especially frightened because she had lost a young brother and a niece to malignant brain tumors. I also felt frightened, but not like Marion. I couldn't believe that our little girl was going to die. I just wouldn't go there.

The next days and weeks were harrowing. Surgery to remove the tumor was delayed because within a week Tanya had developed an infection. The source of the infection was not known, so for a week Tanya ran temperatures that hovered around 104 degrees. Then, one night when Marion was sitting by her bedside, she saw something very strange in Tanya's neck. For just a moment when Tanya sat up and turned her head, Marion noticed a bulge on the side of the neck where the shunt ran from her brain to her abdomen. The bulge was very inflamed and stuck out like a straw which had been bent.

Marion ran to get the doctors but when they examined Tanya, no one could see what Marion had described. Marion couldn't see it anymore either. She felt foolish as it was obvious that the doctors and nurses thought she was imagining things, but the next morning they took Tanya back to surgery to see if there was something wrong with the shunt. They found that they had to remove it, for it had, in fact, become infected. Soon after, the fever broke and, for the first time in a week, we all were able to get some sleep.

We will never know what Marion saw that night. Though we asked the doctors and nurses, no one could explain it. We were simply left with questions no one could answer. Could anyone have seen the same condition if they had been present at the exact time the bulge became visible? Is it possible that Marion, in an intensely heightened state of anxiety was able to transcend our normal human capacity to see? Or, had Marion been granted a gift, a small miracle?

Because Tanya no longer had a shunt to stabilize the flow of spinal fluid, she had to lie flat in bed while the infection cleared. For many days we took turns staying by her bedside, trying to distract her and reassure her that she was going to get well. One Saturday afternoon during that long, tense wait, while Marion was at the hospital and the boys were with my mother, I was at home alone catching up on mundane chores. Actually, the time was providing me with some respite from the struggle of dealing with the logistics of driving to Chicago, finding someone to watch the boys, keeping family informed, and trying to keep up with the work that was piling up at the office. But, about 2:00 p.m. that afternoon it all came crashing down.

I didn't see it coming. As I was getting ready to take a shower, I turned my head and looked into Tanya's bedroom. The afternoon sunlight was coming through the windows and bringing to life her multicolored bedspread which was perfectly made with some new stuffed animals sitting near the pillows waiting for her to come home. The empty room reminded me of the hospital room of another little girl at Children's Hospital who never made it home.

Without warning, I felt hot all over and I knew I was going to be sick. I rushed for the bathroom. I looked up from where I was kneeling on the floor and screamed out to the empty house, "Oh, my God. What if she doesn't make it? What if she dies?"

I had never allowed myself to go there before. Marion had. Marion understood. But I hadn't. I said again to myself, "My God, she could die." Then I just sat there on the floor of that bathroom, shaking and weeping uncontrollably. I couldn't get up. I tried, but I couldn't. Then I began to pray. I prayed the prayer that all parents pray in those times—the bargainer's prayer. I prayed and prayed, "Me. Take me. Please, God, not her. Please, God, not her."

Days and weeks went by. During that time, Tanya was treated for a second infection. Finally, Dr. Raimondi decided to go ahead with the surgery. He did not want to wait as the tumor was continuing to grow and any additional complication could weaken her even more.

The day of the surgery finally came and we sat together, as people do, in that waiting room, not talking about the fear we were feeling. We just sat with rosary beads and prayed for a miracle. After many hours, word finally came: surgery was successful—tumor was benign. She would not need chemotherapy or radiation. She could go home. We were all thrilled and immediately began planning for that happy event, but there was one more hurdle to overcome.

On the day Tanya was supposed to go home, she developed once again a high fever. This time the diagnosis was meningitis. For two more weeks we waited for the medicine to do its work. More than two months after Tanya was first admitted, we assisted a nurse who was placing a very thin, very weak, bald, but happy little girl into a "Let's go Home" wheelchair.

We made two stops on the way home to fulfill promises made during those difficult days—first to get and drink a large chocolate malt at Peter's restaurant and next to stop at a shop to pick out a wig. It was different from the thick, long, honey brown color of her own hair, but for her in that moment it was better than having no hair at all. Then we were on our way to our home, back yard, brothers, and stuffed animals that were waiting patiently on a little girl's bed.

The gift that I shall forever cherish is the picture I hold of her as she so very carefully ventured out into our sunlit back yard. She was so weak that she nearly stumbled on the uneven grass as she walked from the house toward her favorite massive oak trees. She looked back with a smile that filled the whole world. But her eyes are what I shall most vividly remember and hold forever close to my heart. They shone with a joy that is reserved only for the totally innocent and pure—a gift given by God, delivered by guardian angels to those chosen to see the world in a very special way—a gift I was allowed to witness and cherish to this day.

Life is so very fragile, but every moment we have is filled with gifts that God has placed in our lives for us to cherish—the finest of these gifts are the simplest, like an unsteady walk in a sunlit backyard and the smile on the face of one of God's chosen.

"The person who works desires not only due remuneration for his work; he also wishes that, within the production process, provisions be made for him to be able to know that in his work, even on something that is owned in common, he is working 'for himself.' This awareness is extinguished within him in a system of excessive bureaucratic centralization, which makes the worker feel that he is just a cog in a huge machine moved from above..."

Encyclical Laborem exercens

Section 15 the "Personalist" argument, 8-11

Pope John Paul II

CHAPTER FOURTEEN

A New Understanding

I was raised in a working-class family. My grandfathers, father, and uncles all worked with their hands and backs. So, I heard stories of the work houses and steel plants from my earliest childhood days. But the stories I heard were of men who worked in the cruelest of non-union settings.

After World War II, unions had become powerful enough to cause conditions in union workplaces to be greatly improved, but in the non-union workplace, conditions were still very demanding, very harsh, and very unsafe. Workers were poorly paid, worked long hours without breaks, and were inadequately protected from accidents. If they complained or couldn't keep up with the demands of their task, they were easily and readily replaced.

From a young age, I also worked with my hands and back. Thus, you might think that I would have understood what those who preceded me had experienced. But I did not, for times had changed. I did not know that these brutal conditions still existed anywhere. Not until my work experience at JT Steel Corporation did a true depth of empathy and understanding take hold.

Although I did not know it when I went to work at that factory, my God was about to push me headlong into an experience that I needed to have so that I could understand and advocate for the humane and dignified treatment of workers wherever they toiled. I did not know, at that time, that much of my future life's work would focus in large part on speaking to large groups about ways to insure workers are valued and appropriately rewarded for their contributions.

Some people, of course, would see the experience at JT Steel Corporation, as simply an accident borne out of need to find any kind of job in order to help take care of a family. Others, including me, would come to see that experience as what God wanted me to have in order for the steel of my soul to be appropriately tempered.

The story, *Lift that Bale*, which follows has been adapted from an earlier book, *Sweet Land of Liberty*, which we published in 2011.

****

In the late 1950s the steel companies across the United States had been running 24 hours a day and stockpiling steel in anticipation of a national steel strike predicted to be of extraordinary length. I was attending St. Joseph's College, in East Chicago, but I and many of my classmates understood that college days might soon come to an abrupt end. My father was a steel worker. Soon all family resources would be needed for food, heat, and other bills that had to be paid.

When the strike finally did start, it struck like a sledge hammer. Virtually all unnecessary purchases were stopped. Though people could drive their cars to the grocery store, church, and the doctor, they walked. People hoarded money, using it only for essentials, as it was understood that this strike would be a long and bitter one. Those out of work because of the strike would take work of any kind.

The third week into the strike, I got lucky. While walking from plant to plant near Whiting and the north side of Hammond, I landed a job. JT Steel Corporation, some four miles from my home, was looking for two laborers. I filled out the application in their employment office and turned it in.

"You didn't fill out when you could start, kid."

"When do you need me?"

"Now."

"Then I'm ready."

They let me make a quick phone call home. I took my tie off, rolled up the sleeves of my white shirt and hit the slippery, greased-soaked floor of the plant ready to work. I had a job.

I had worked factory jobs before at Standard Forge, Youngstown Steel, and Inland Steel in East Chicago. But here at JT Steel, without union support, I would soon find that this would be a work experience of a kind that I could never have imagined. Immediately, I found a total lack of any safety standards. Grease, grime, and filth were everywhere, and fearless rats the size of large cats ran wild. When they showed their teeth you gave them a wide berth, and you learned quickly never to get trapped working in the dark end of a boxcar with them between you and the only boxcar door.

The intense and constant noise from the massive presses never stopped except when a worker's hand or arm was crushed in the machinery. This was not infrequent because workers who were being paid on piece work were always attempting to beat the odds for a few dollars more. Setting aside the safety harnesses worn to protect them from such accidents was common and when observed by supervisors nothing was said. Increasing productivity was a primary company goal. When the inevitable occurred, it was for me the most frightening and terrifying of moments.

The first time I saw it happen, I knew the kid who was hurt. His name was Jessie; he was 22, had a wife and a child, and had come from Alabama for work. When we got a lunch break, he would eat his sandwich quickly then pull out his guitar and play some ballad from home. Part of my job was to keep Jessie supplied with the parts he needed in order to continuously feed his assigned press. The memory of his accident will never leave me. The sound that the press makes when it crushes human bone is a sound you remember for the rest of your life. I helped other workers attempt to create a makeshift tourniquet in order to stop the spraying of blood. There was, however, no way to stop his screaming, and our prayers were that he would soon pass out from the pain. But he didn't.

During my third week of work, we had been on a dead run since 7:00 a.m. It was now noon. The temperature in the plant was near 105 degrees. The lunch whistle blew and the kid next to me dropped to his knees then wiped his brow with his work glove.

The foreman came over to him and said, "You there, get back on your feet. You guys aren't done."

The kid said, "The lunch bell just rang."

"There ain't no lunch for you guys today. You're behind. You work faster tomorrow, you eat. Today you work till you catch up."

The kid got up, looked at the foreman and said, "Bullshit. I'm gonna eat."

The foreman then pointed at him and said, "You're fired. Outta here."

From noon till 1:30 p.m. I worked alone. By then a new kid had been hired. There were always six or seven guys waiting on an old bench in the sun outside of the employment office hoping for a break. I felt bad for the guy who got fired, also for the new kid in the white shirt with the rolled-up sleeves. He'd never get the grease out of that shirt. I had one hanging in my closet just like it at home.

The non-union experience was incongruent with my understanding of the work place. Unfortunately, I was the only one in our family working, so I needed the job. I found myself taking a lot of abuse for fear of losing the job. It wasn't a good feeling. My only salvation was my understanding that I would not have to spend my lifetime of work here. At some point the national steel strike would be over, Dad would be back at work, and I could return to college. This was not the understanding of my colleagues in that plant. They were there for the duration of their lives. The thought of this was unbearable.

The worst for me came one day toward the end of my third month of work. The temperature in the plant that day exceeded 130 degrees on the upper floor near the tin roof where steel was stored in large bins and needed to be shoveled into large wooden boxes below. I was shoveling up there alone, and I had been at it for about two hours.

I was beginning to cramp and my clothes were soaked. Even the insides of my shoes were soaked from the sweat running down my legs. Other workers would be coming for the loaded boxes in 15 minutes. I knew I could finish filling the boxes in 10 minutes and then catch a five minute break, or instead of a break, I could use the five minutes to run to the bathroom near the locker room—something I had been holding off doing, but couldn't any longer.

With the strength of my arms alone, I moved my trembling legs down the wooden ladder, but then I began to cramp badly. Finally, I just hung there not able to go up or down. Losing control, I began to urinate. I hung onto that ladder, urinating, cramping, and weeping at the same time. Anger was filling my whole soul while shame waited its turn.

Five minutes later I managed to get off of the ladder and was again shoveling, filling the next empty boxes. I vowed to myself that I would fill those boxes until I dropped. I was distancing myself from those I worked for. My anger was turning to bitterness. I began to understand how camaraderie and good feelings between employees and employers could be crushed.

As importantly, I was learning how easily brotherly love could have been preserved. I understood that this bitterness could have been overcome had I encountered one, only one, supervisor interested in my value and dignity as a human being.

****

The tempered steel of my soul was ready.

As I said earlier in this chapter, there are those who would believe that my finding the job at JT steel was pure chance. I never will. Though I did not have any idea what His later plans for me would be, God did. And He understood what I would need to perform that work.

Therefore, though not of my choosing, "On My Way Home, I Bumped into God."

"'Master, which is the greatest commandment in the law?' Jesus said to him: 'Thou shalt love thy Lord thy God with thy whole Heart, and with thy whole soul, and with thy whole mind. This is the greatest and first commandment. And the second is like to this: Thou shalt love thy neighbor as thyself. On these two commandments dependeth the whole law and the Prophets.'"

Matthew 22:36-40

CHAPTER FIFTEEN

A Meaningful Life

Like most college students of my day and background, I had no clear understanding as to what I wanted to do with my life. I did not know how to create a life that would be meaningful. I was fairly directionless. The steel mills were an option. They were close by, paid well, and jobs seemed secure. But my parents, as many parents of those days, wanted more for me. So, I and other young people like me attended a newly-created Catholic community college with virtually no understanding of our intended purpose. Many of us worked midnight shifts in one of the many mills in that industrial area and then during the days went to our classes, oftentimes, straight from work with our metatarsal shoes still on.

In the evenings we occasionally went to local workmen's bars down the street from the college and sometimes drank too much. The only skills we seemed to be acquiring were shooting darts or scoring on the bowling shuffleboard tables in the back of those bars.

Only a few of our number seemed to know where they wanted life to take them and we often demeaned those who did, challenging the wisdom of their intended direction. I think now that many of us, including me, envied them. One of these students was Big Ed.

Big Ed

Ed was only a sophomore and hadn't been at our college very long. When he began to attend, he drove in from Michigan City every day to our store-front college in downtown East Chicago. He was a big guy and God had blessed him with such a calm and forgiving nature it was almost impossible to get Ed mad. Even in the concluding moments of our most heated philosophical or political arguments as we sat on the edges of our seats around one of the tables in the back of George's Diner, Ed would look up, smile and with his warm, engaging eyes say something like, "If that's how you see it, God Bless you." His charismatic smile, coupled with his soft look and tone, was absolutely disarming.

He had only one unshakable purpose in going to college. He wanted to be a social worker and give his life to helping others, or as he would say, "helping people who just never got my breaks." In his free time, primarily in Michigan City near his home, he organized food drives. At our college he helped collect winter coats for kids. His clear focus was helping his fellow man, especially kids, and he never seemed to tire of doing it.

His way of doing things was contagious, so if you spent any time at all with Ed you found yourself helping before you even knew you were involved. It never felt, when working with Ed, that what you were doing was a chore. You enjoyed it because he enjoyed it, and when the task was finished, he made you feel like your assistance alone had been the decisive factor in bringing about the success of the venture.

It was about three o'clock in the afternoon on a very cold and snowy day in mid-December. The lake-effect snow had been coming off of Lake Michigan since midnight. Most of us were in the small, newly-constructed library that had a large picture window looking out onto Indianapolis Boulevard. Prior to the college's existence, the building had been a furniture store. A lot of us were fixated on trying to see out of this front window, but the wind and snow were blowing so hard that it was nearly impossible to catch more than a glimpse of the street even though it was just some ten feet away.

Suddenly, the front door opened and, bringing in with him a rush of snow, our classmate Marty stood there motionless, the door ajar behind him. Maybe because of the way he just stood there so quietly, or maybe it was because of the look on his face, I'm not sure, but we all knew something was wrong, really wrong. Then he told us.

Ed was dead. Marty explained that Ed had given a friend a ride to Rensselaer, Indiana that morning, and on his way back to St. Joseph's he had gotten caught in the winter storm, slid off the road, hit an embankment, and died instantly. No one spoke. Some of us just sat there and allowed the tears to run down our cheeks and dampen out shirts.

It was a short walk to the Little Catholic Church of Immaculate Conception on the corner, a block off of the Boulevard. It was dark in the church except for the warm and ever-present glow of the red flickering vigil light hanging over the altar. No one

131

spoke. Finally, Tobias pulled out his rosary and began to pray. We reflexively followed. I'm not sure how many decades we said. But no one wanted to stop because we knew that when we did, we would break down and none of us were ready for that. None of us could stop the dark, angry thoughts.

All we could think about was that Big Ed was dead and we felt, somehow, that God had no right to do that. Ed was one of the few who knew what he wanted to do with his life. He was going to do good things and now those good things weren't going to happen. God shouldn't have done that—not to Ed.

It's so predictable when such an unanticipated disaster occurs that we somehow blame God. In a sense, we are like the small child who falls, but when picked up by a parent who tries to comfort him, clenches his fist and strikes out at the parent as if he were somehow responsible. After a while, he rests his head on the parent's shoulder and asks for help to make the pain go away, never understanding that the parent's pain for him was more intense than his own.

God was kneeling with us in that church that day. His eyes also filled with tears while he prayed with us. We just weren't ready yet to put our head on His shoulder and ask for His help to make the pain go away. We weren't quite ready to bump into God.

Moving On

We seem able to deal best with death if the loved one had the opportunity for a long and productive life and we could hold his hand as he passed. Anything less than that can be emotionally devastating. We don't really get over it. The trust we carried with us from our childhood is gone. We are confronted with the raw fact that death can happen to us or anyone we know, it can happen at any time, and it can happen without the comfort of a friend or a loved one. For those of us who grieved for the loss of Big Ed, the world was now a less joyful and less secure place. It was a place we couldn't easily count on, and planning for the future now had a large question mark—one that hadn't been quite so prominent before. While he was with us, Ed had held the baton outstretched. He had declared his commitment to a better world, and he had said it often. Could we—should we—grab hold and run in his place?

The semesters drifted by. Good things and not such good things happened. The college purchased another building, some of us took on leadership roles in the new student council, and the library got bigger. Metatarsal work shoes wore out and had to be replaced. Some were replaced with regular shoes. The coursework got more challenging and the halls were filling with students who had never known Big Ed. The coffee breaks at George's Diner stayed the same, and often, without explanation, we intentionally left a chair around the table empty.

Graduations had started to thin our ranks. A few left for Chicago and graduate school. Some went into teaching. Jerry and I were finishing in business and economics. It was about time for us to go. And anyway, we really couldn't get up a good football game at the park anymore—not enough guys interested in playing on frozen ground. Foreign beers and wines had become preferred drinks at the bars adjacent to the college, so we had to walk three or four blocks to the tracks and the roundhouse area to find a good bar. Yes, it was time to go.

Yet, for me, the question was still unresolved. Would I be able to direct my life into the rich experience that Ed in his young heart had been prepared and ready for? Could I find something that I could commit to? Could I grab the baton and just run, not even knowing where the run would take me? I didn't know. Could I continue the run even when I got older and no longer had the gift of strength given to the young? I didn't know.

I had purchased my cap and gown and was ready to graduate, but three days before graduation I got a call from the a dean at the college advising me that I was one course short for my economics degree. The next two days my hours were filled with anger and anxiety. I was lost. What I was going to do next? Eventually, I began to make a new plan. I made a change in majors and enrolled. Several days later, as I was polishing my work shoes, I received an unanticipated phone call.

"Ray?"

"Yes."

"Ray, this is Phil. Word on the street is that you're gonna be around for awhile. Is that right?"

"Yeah, Phil, I thought I was finished, but I found out that I needed one more course to graduate. Nothing I can do about it but take the course."

"Well, listen, Ray, while you are taking that course would you like to coach football?"

"Phil, what do you mean coach football?"

"Well actually it's more than coaching football. It's also teaching seventh grade in Schererville at St. Michael's. They just lost their seventh grade teacher unexpectedly, and they also lost their football coach just three days ago. He is being transferred out of state by his company. I just accepted a job teaching fifth grade at the school for this fall, and in a meeting this morning with a few of the parishioners and the pastor, Fr. Duty, a lot of names were suggested. When Fr. Duty saw your name on the list, he brightened up and asked, 'Can you get him?' He apparently knows of you through Fr. Heeg and some of the priests at St. Joe College. So I was appointed to make the preliminary call. Will you do it?"

I remember being thoroughly stunned, and then said, "But Phil, I have never taken an education course in my life. I'm not licensed. I don't even have a college degree, and I have never coached football, just played it."

"Ray, you just don't get it, do you? The pastor wants you."

I decided I would take a chance on this opportunity, and that decision changed my life. My Dad gave me his coach's whistle which he used when he coached my eighth grade football team, and in mid-August I met my team on the Schererville athletic field. I never thought that I could enjoy work that much. I found that it was a daily pleasure both on the field and in the classroom. I had 44 students and taught math, English, social studies, religion, spelling, science, penmanship, history, geography, and music.

A fourth of my students were bussed in daily from Fr. Campagna's home for neglected and delinquent boys. I enjoyed them all thoroughly and they did nothing but add to the strength of the football team. A lot of girls were always hanging around our football practice at the park with nothing to do. So, with the permission of the school and their parents, I started the first track team for girls. I was having a ball.

I had found something that I could commit to, or rather, it had found me. As I reflected on how everything had taken place, I came to believe that I didn't have much to do with it at all. Most of us are taught throughout our lives that we are in charge and that we control what happens to us. *I think we control very little.* If we pray and ask for help, the help comes, but not necessarily in the manner and form requested. It comes, rather, in the manner and form that the Creator understands is in our best interest.

I spent the next 43 years on the path that had opened up for me. I taught middle school and high school, worked with delinquents and delinquent gangs. For over ten years, I taught philosophy, psychology, and sociology to college students and, in addition, specialized courses to law enforcement officers from Chicago. As an administrator, I directed the operations of special education, counseling and nursing staffs, and then took on the responsibilities of assistant superintendent, and superintendent of schools. For many years I traveled to conferences where I gave the keynote speech. Little, if any, of that run was planned— by me.

Over the long years of my career, I often reflected particularly on Big Ed as I was keynoting educational conferences and attempting to advise teachers and administrators about the noble goals of their profession. I felt I was helping people as the audiences were immensely receptive and appreciative, frequently giving me standing ovations. I was turning down more requests than I was accepting. I was on a mission and I was invincible—or so I thought. The first time I hit the wall, I didn't even see it coming.

Shattering

All up and down the east coast there were severe storms. The rain was turning into ice. All flights were being cancelled, and I had been stuck in the Charlotte airport most of the day. This was the fourth day of a five-day trip during which I was going to have to crisscross the country twice, keynoting conferences from Vancouver to Miami. The weather had been rotten since the day I left home and flights had not been anywhere near on time all week.

I hadn't eaten yet and was soaking wet from sweat. I had begun to get the shakes several hours earlier and they were getting worse. I had some anxiety meds, but I was saving them to take when I went to bed. If I didn't reserve them for that time, I was afraid I might not be able to sleep again. That would be the third night in a row that I would be unable to get needed rest.

The airport was an ant hill that was on fire. Down the hall, I could see a guy in total frustration and anger trying to kick a phone booth off of the wall. I drew back, took a deep breath and watched countless human beings, out of control and running around aimlessly. I was frightened to understand that I was a part of it.

I took another deep breath, grabbed my bag, went out of the airport, and took a cab to the nicest Marriott I could find. I checked in, took a hot shower, ordered their best steak for room service, turned off all of the lights, and opened the drapes wide. As I watched what was now a storm of sleet and swirling snow, I slowly ate my steak. I didn't wake until 11:00 a.m. the next morning. When I awoke, I found that I was still in the chair. The storm outside had passed. But mine had just begun.

People who travel and work, spending no more than a day or two in one place, are a special breed. Members of this breed are especially vulnerable if, during those temporary stops, the task is to entertain or enlighten large audiences sometimes numbering over a thousand. There's no opportunity to say, "Wait a minute. Let's start again," or "I'm a little tired right now, how about this afternoon?" So, as age creeps up and sleep is erratic, anxiety grows, especially after going through another "almost-didn't-make-the-flight "episode. Then stronger anti-anxiety and sleeping pills are not only useless, they can cause side effects that make presenting difficult.

One of the side effects for me was extreme dizziness. I found that as I was sitting on the stage in front of a large audience waiting to be introduced, I would get very dizzy and knew that if I stood, I could easily fall. Thus, it became routine for me to ask the person who would be introducing me to come over to me and shake my hand after he finished. We would then continue to shake hands until he or she could get me to the podium where

I could let go and hold onto the podium until the condition passed. That way the audience would never know. I developed any number of these little tricks. They became essential if I was going to continue.

The worst and most depressing parts of the day began after the keynotes were finished, and once again the long periods of being alone began—alone as I left the conference, alone on the trip to the airport, alone as I waited for planes, alone in a new hotel, alone as I made the all too brief phone calls to home, alone in a new hotel room, in a different bed—alone—over and over again.

As the years drifted by, the confidence that I was doing good things began to dissipate. There was little time for interaction or interactive feedback. The courage and personal inner strength that was in such abundance in my youth began to crumble. Some entertainers or presenters drink when this happens or they do drugs, or some find solace in brief encounters. Some look for better and more effective medications. Some pray.

One day I began to travel to a speaking engagement. It was not a particularly unusual day, simply a day set aside to fly. My first flight to St. Louis was unremarkable. It wasn't until I got off of the plane in St. Louis and began to walk to the gate for my second flight that the anxiety went up to a new level and hit like walking full-speed into an anvil. The distance which could not have been more than several hundred yards to the next gate looked to be miles long, and I could not stop perspiring nor shaking. I found a bathroom, went into a vacant stall, sat, and just prayed. It didn't help. I knew that I couldn't stay there forever, I'd miss my flight.

The anxiety attack was full-blown during the second flight all the way to touchdown in Little Rock. I was soaking wet. At the gate, I was met by a long time friend. His presence, his warm conversation, and our shared dinner did a lot to alleviate the intense anxiety I was feeling. Though the upscale hotel and lovely room were comforting, I knew it would be a sleepless night—I was too wired. But, I had done this many times before, and my only obligation tomorrow was the introductory keynote at 10:00 in the morning—a piece of cake.

I pulled out my rosary after a warm shower and lay down in the dim light. I prayed what we called the street kid's prayer— more a conversation with God than a series of standard requests. Was it time to hang up my spikes? Was I out here just making money? Had it ever been anything other than making money? Was I making a difference for any one? Had I ever made a difference? My conversation was a series of questions that I seemed to be repeating over and over again throughout the long night. Finally, I remember feeling some unanticipated calm and ended my prayer with, "Look, God, if you can give me some kind of sign, this would be a good time." Dim morning light was beginning to come through the drawn and covered windows. I dozed off.

Rescued

I had a light breakfast in the hotel restaurant. My stomach told me I couldn't handle any more food. Then I headed to the conference area. The room was filling and there would soon be eight-to-nine hundred persons seated in the audience. I sat in my place on the stage behind the podium as I had done so often before, but this time was different. The questions of doubt, only infrequent in the past, filled and raced through my mind. Did any of this matter? By tomorrow, would anyone even remember that I was here or even remember anything of what I had said? Was this all simply a huge waste of time?

As these questions raced through my mind, I saw a man coming through the crowd toward the stage. He was very well-dressed, a big man about my age. As he approached, he looked at me with his warm engaging eyes and smiled. As I continued to watch him approach, it was clear from his bearing that he was at peace inside and he knew it. As he came closer, I could see that he was coming directly to me. I stood. He graciously clasped my hand with his hands and said,

"Dr. Golarz, I'm sure you don't remember me. Please forgive me for bothering you before you speak but I was afraid later you would not be available and I had something I needed you to know. My name is Matt Brown. I am a superintendent here in Arkansas. I left home at 5:00 a.m. this morning so that I would make it in time to see you and again hear you."

I was overwhelmed and said, "Please, please. Matt, is it? What did you want to say?"

He then continued, "Ten years ago I had just become superintendent and I heard you speak at a School Improvement Conference in Phoenix. What you said about the dignity of teachers and staff and their need to be treated with honor and respect changed my life and affected the manner in which I treated all of my people for all of these years. We have a wonderful and caring school district now—a place of dignity where we emphasize the worth of people. I hope you don't mind my coming up right now like this, but I just needed you to know that."

There are probably only a few times in life when we are totally disarmed, when all of the bones of our body simply turn to jelly. This was one of those times. I was speechless and touched in the innermost parts of my soul.

He then asked, "Dr Golarz?" I finally answered, "Matt, I simply can't tell you what that meant to me." He nodded, shook my hand again, smiled, and left the stage.

I just stood there. What could I speak about now? I had been ready to give the speech I had prepared, but no longer could I do that. What could I have said to that audience ten years ago that meant so much to Matt? How could I now present this keynote and chance missing the mark? What if there is someone else out there who really needs to hear me say something really significant and I don't come through? These thoughts raced through my mind—good thoughts, the kind I hadn't had for a long time. So, I prayed for guidance and trusted that it would come. As I was introduced and approached the podium it still wasn't clear, but somehow I knew it would be. So I put my trust in God and started:

"My dear friends and colleagues, Today, I'd like to tell you some stories that are close to my heart. Stories of people who wanted to make a difference. Let me start with a story that takes me way back. Let me tell you about Big Ed."

I had never before given a presentation like that, nor have I done so since. It was done only that once for a very special time, and, I think, for a very special reason.

On the way home that day in cabs, airports, planes and waiting areas, I didn't feel quite so alone. And since that day I have never had that same sense of being alone. Possibly that is because I no longer believe that I am. As matter of fact, the older I get, the less I believe that any of us is alone. I think our God is there all of the time, just patiently waiting for us to look into His eyes so that He can smile back and give us peace. On that day, I think I had again bumped into God.

Whether or not I have completely and consistently honored the second part of the greatest commandment given us—to love our neighbor as we love ourselves is a question I continually ask myself. But, I know that through the love and nudging of God and models like Big Ed I stumbled my way into the spirit of that command. Maybe that's all any of us can do in order to build a meaningful life.

The third question in the Baltimore Catechism is, "Why did God make you?" The response to this question is, "God made us to show forth his goodness and to share with us His everlasting happiness in heaven." The question and its response were never intended to frighten us. The intention was rather to provide for us hope and joy.

But as we all know, in order for us to share this everlasting happiness in Heaven we must first die, and for virtually all human beings to die is frightening. It is the ultimate leap of faith, and it usually scares us. It can cease being frightening if we are surrounded by prayer, the sacraments, or if someone whom we trust and love is getting ready to make the leap themselves, smiles and says to us with their eyes, "Relax. Everything is going to be okay."

CHAPTER SIXTEEN

A Brotherly Nudge

In addition to his captivating smile, Joe was blessed with the skills that made him a natural athlete at virtually any sport he decided to try. Whether it was ice hockey, football, basketball, golf or baseball, he played them well. Golf was the game he played best. Only the angels have a swing like that.

Joe did have an obsession that I must confess also got me into a lot of trouble. He was unable to control his anger when he saw an unfair fight, and because of where we grew up, there were lots of unfair fights. I recall one of his confrontations at the golf course on a hot July day. An extremely big kid, who later in life became a professional wrestler, was picking on someone much smaller than he was. Joe warned him to stop. Instead, the big kid struck the smaller boy on the side of the head, knocking him violently to the ground. Joe didn't hesitate. He immediately punched the kid hard. I was amazed to see that the blow had hit its mark because the kid was so tall that Joe actually had to jump up to hit him. The bully ran away from Joe in tears.

Unfortunately, Joe's righteous mission to secure justice was not always something he could handle alone. That's where I, reluctantly, came in. By the time I was 13, I had lost count of the crusades he had dragged me into. It's not that his interventions weren't justified, they were simply so many. Once over the dinner table, even my father noticed some bruises and remarked to me. "Ray, you seem to be getting banged up a lot." "Yes, Dad, just not being careful enough, I guess." Joe nearly choked on his mouthful of food trying not to laugh. I'm sure I kicked him under the table.

Joe's sense of justice didn't always show because of an unfair fight. When I was about 13 and Joe about 10 years old, Dad took us to a football game. The game was a battle of high school titans, and it was well-attended with a crowd of more than 5,000 fans. Sometime during the hot and humid third quarter, the home team called a time out. Virtually all of the players on both teams went down on a knee. As they did, the water boy from the home team's bench came running at full speed. When he got to within ten feet of the resting players, he tripped and fell. His arms and legs seemed to go in every direction as did his water bottles. The entire crowd, less one, roared.

Joe sat motionless between Dad and me. His left hand was on his heart and a tear was streaming down his face. Then without looking at either of us he whispered, "That poor kid."

That was one of the strongest nudges I had received to that point in my life. How had my younger brother seen what I had not? How had he seen what no one in that crowd had seen? I vowed that I would never again react to someone's embarrassing situation with such a lack of sensitivity.

Many years later Joe developed lung cancer. By the time the diagnosis was confirmed, the cancer was very advanced. As the end was approaching, a priest was called and the Sacrament of the Sick was administered. I wanted very badly to be with Joe, but he asked of us that we not make the long trip to the upper reaches of Michigan to see him. "I'll be okay, he insisted."

Those are the trips that are the longest trips of all. There is a lifetime of memories to sort through when you are going to be with a loved one who is dying. In the case of Joe, the memories went way back. I didn't want the experiences that created those memories to ever be over. Like most people in that situation, I cried a lot as we were driving, but I was comforted by my loving wife who understood when to talk and when to say nothing.

When we finally got to be with Joe, we found him sitting in a chair. It was obvious he had trouble holding his head up because of the pain and heavy medication he was taking. But he did raise his head, looked into my eyes and smiled. I had seen that particular look in his eyes on only one other occasion. It was when we were caddies, and he was holding a sobbing boy over a railroad track in his arms.

I knew in my heart those many years ago that Joe was not alone. I knew then that the love and compassion shining through my brother's eyes were not coming from only him. He had those many years ago been with his God, and he was now with his God again. In that moment, out of the deep capacity of his love for me, he told me with his smile and his eyes, "Hey, Ray, relax. Everything is okay."

The next day Marion and I drove home. I never saw my little brother again. I know that someday I will. I know it because with his eyes and his smile he told me so. So, in my quiet moments I sometimes just close my eyes and watch him swing. Eventually he turns my way, and from the edge of the 18th. green he smiles at me, and with my eyes still closed, I smile back.

As I continue the latter part of my life's walk, Joe's endearing smile that I find just by closing my eyes is one of the encounters with God that I most treasure.

As a young boy growing up in a culture which embraced the Roman Catholic faith, I came to love many of the religious traditions that were built into our daily lives. Blended with the warmth, love, and faith with which my parents and grandparents surrounded me was the sharing of my grandmother's devotion to saying the rosary in the Polish language which was musical to me. It is a practice I still hold in reverence today as I am relearning that special way of praying.

CHAPTER SEVENTEEN

Seeds and Beads

From the time I was very young, I saw signs of God's existence everywhere I looked. I am sure I was more aware of them during World War II because of the never-ending anxiety that dominated our lives. However, even after the war ended, I found that I was still surrounded by religious items. They were as much a part of my life as enjoying the food on our table, being with family, playing with my brother, or seeing the sunlight coming in through the windows.

I couldn't enter my house or my Busia's house without seeing a crucifix on a living room wall, or palms from Palm Sunday placed behind a picture or the chalk etchings at the top of the front door frames where the priests had written the names of the Three Kings as they performed their annual blessings. Both homes had a number of statues. Mom's favorite was a statue of the Infant of Prague that she always prominently displayed on a corner table in the dining room. My Busia preferred to display the Blessed Virgin. In both homes candles were periodically lit to celebrate some special feast, or to aid in seeking guidance or to ask for their intercession in times of anxiety or peril.

We didn't have a lot of books, but the Bible, catechisms, and missals for Mass were always within easy reach. The *Sunday Visitor*, the Polish newspaper (*Dziennik Zwiazkowy*), and the *Ligourian magazine* were always in plain view on a chair, table, or couch. Rosaries and scapulars could be located easily by opening any top drawer of any piece of furniture in the dining room or bedrooms. Holy water could be found on both mom's and Busia's bedroom dresser. Like I said, the signs were everywhere.

Like most kids, I loved rosary beads. They were beautiful to look at. I liked to hold them and feel the textures and sizes of the various beads, and if the beads were made of crystal, they would sparkle like little prisms. From the time I was very young, they were used with prayers, said in a language that to my ears was enchanting and soothing. Joe became so taken with the rosary that as a young seminarian he became extremely good at making them. He became so skilled that he was commissioned to make a special rosary for the wedding of the queen of Belgium. It was a work of art.

Busia was devoted to saying the rosary. In the evenings as we relaxed in her living room, she would be seated in her favorite chair. While Joe, sometimes Barbara, and I would sit or lie on the floor in front of the radio, engrossed in some program such as *Superman* or the *Green Hornet*, Busia would be fingering her beads.

Occasionally, during the day I would find her kneeling at the foot of her bed in her bedroom. If I looked in, she might motion for me to come in. For the time that it took to say a decade or part of one, she had me kneel next to her and hold the rosary with her. Praying with Busia was not forced. I could come in, pray a little, and then leave if I wished. When I was with her, I noticed that she prayed a little louder. I'm sure that was for my benefit. Her prayers were always said in Polish and I loved the rhythm, especially the middle section of the Hail Mary which was said ten times in each decade. I could understand some of the prayer, but not all.

In the introduction of the book, I said that God's back-up plan was multifaceted. That multifaceted approach includes, I believe, the planting of seeds in the hearts of little children. The seed most strongly implanted in me was the memory of kneeling next to Busia and listening to that magical sound of the Hail Mary, said over and over again in a foreign, yet familiar, language.

As a young child, I heard the Polish language being spoken, but I didn't hear it long enough to become fluent. It wasn't until quite recently that I came back to that language, mostly as a consequence of my many conversations with my Aunt Rose, Busia's youngest daughter. Prior to her death, she assisted Marion and me in a publication titled *Sweet Land of Liberty*. Because she still spoke Polish fluently, she was especially helpful with names of people, places and events. Our discussion reminded me of how much I loved that language. I think this is why I was compelled to go back and study Polish, especially the language used in prayers. I studied those prayers until eventually I was learning to say them again in Polish, the way I first heard them.

First I relearned *The Sign of the Cross*, then *The Angel Prayer* and then *The Hail Mary*. As I became more and more proficient, the rhythms and mystical sounds began to return, not now from the lips of Busia, or my father, or my mother, but from me. As I sat at my desk in my bedroom at times in twilight dim, the experience was intoxicating. Seeds planted in the heart of the little child were now sprouting in the heart a grown man.

My favorite rosary is one given to Marion by our daughter Jocelyn. It was a rosary that she brought back and presented to her mother from a long ago trip to Rome. It is a sweet, almost childlike rosary with clear red beads. Relearning *The Our Father* in Polish was quite a challenge, but last year I sat at my desk and with that red rosary completed my very first, five-decade rosary in Polish. I believe that Busia and my Aunt Rose even now are enjoying that.

Last month I mailed tapes that I recorded of *The Sign of the Cross* and *The Angel Prayer* in Polish to my daughter who now lives in upper Pennsylvania and to my son who lives in Philadelphia. Together they have four young children ranging in ages from two to ten. Perhaps someday I will hear them say the rosary, whether it be in Polish or English. I know my mother and father, along with my grandparents, uncles and aunts would enjoy that. I am sure that I would enjoy that too.

Seeds and beads—good back-up plan, God.

*The poem which begins the following chapter was "accidentally" rediscovered while reviewing some poetry which had been written and set aside many years ago. While the inspiration for the poem was the celebration of an earthly home, it became immediately obvious that the meaning was uniquely transformed when placed in the context of the ideas we are exploring in this book-**a coincidence or just another "bump" from God?***

Chapter Eighteen

"You're Welcome Here Inside"

And where do you call home, young man?

    Is it near or is it far,

        Nestled in a forest,

            Or somewhere near a star?

Oh, it has a big front porch, you say,

    With a window open wide

        And lights that say to passers-by

        You're welcome here inside.

Then you are never lost, my lamb,

    No matter where you be.

        Just close your eyes and sail there

        Through lovely memories.

—Marion Golarz

The typical dictionary definition of the word home begins with the obvious physical characteristics of this concept. It is a place where one lives as in a house or apartment; it's the physical structure within which one lives. But in the context of what we have written and suggested in this book the meaning of home is much more profound, for we are talking about the place where our souls will finally be able to rest in the love of God.

Although we associate being in our heavenly home with complete happiness, we are not sure that we understand all the reasons for that happiness. We have been promised that we will know the majesty of God and that we will be surrounded by the beautiful voices of angels. But, we think God, in his infinite wisdom, knows our inherent need to seek a place where we are safe, where we fit, where we are not alone, where we will once again reunite in forgiveness and love with the other souls who walked with us on our earthly journey. This is the kind of home our souls, at their core, remember and seek to return to from the moment of our birth. This is the place God has prepared for us—a place where we are never lost, a place where we are welcome, a place we can sail to by just closing our eyes one last time.

About the Authors

Marion J. Golarz was born in Conneaut, Ohio to Marion and Michael Simpson. She was the sixth of seven children. As a child she attended St. Mary's School. After securing her B.S. in English Language Arts from Indiana University, she taught at Bishop Noll High School near Chicago. After securing an M.S. with certification in the area of reading from Indiana University, she worked for the Title I program as a reading teacher helping elementary, middle school and high school students who needed remedial instruction.

At Purdue Calumet and Indiana University East she taught English composition and enjoyed working with students in the writing lab at Purdue Calumet. She has presented at conferences throughout the country. Working in various venues with teachers, parents, and administrators, she presented research, book reviews, and led discussions on educational topics.

With her husband of 49 years, Raymond, she has co-authored *The Power of Participation,* and *Sweet Land of Liberty.* Together she and Raymond have six children: Tanya Scherschel, Michael Golarz, Dr. Scott Golarz, Jocelyn Golarz, Daniel Golarz and Thomas John Golarz. They presently have seven grandchildren.

Marion is an avid reader and lover of good writing. She currently resides in Bloomington, Indiana with Raymond and their two cats Lucky and Patches. Life remains full.

Raymond J Golarz was born in East Chicago, Indiana to Helen and John (Lefty) Golarz. He was one of five children. His early childhood was split between living in East Hammond, Indiana and in Hessville, Indiana. Thus, as a child he attended both St. Mary's and Our Lady of Perpetual Help elementary schools. For the first two years of high school, he attended Our Lady of the Lake Seminary in Indiana and as a college student he attended St. Lawrence Seminary in Wisconsin.

After securing his B.A. and B.S. degrees from St. Joseph's College in Indiana, and an M.S. from Indiana University, he taught and coached at Saint Michael's school and Bishop Noll high school where he met Marion. He later secured his Ed.D. from Indiana University and then served as the Director of Child Welfare Services, supervising delinquency prevention and intervention programs and working with delinquent gangs and drug intervention programs. At the college level, he taught psychology and sociology courses at St. Joseph's College, Purdue Calumet, Indiana University Northwest. For ten years, he enjoyed teaching psychology near Chicago to law enforcement officers. At City College in Seattle, Washington, he taught master level education courses. He has served as an assistant superintendent and superintendent of public schools and has keynoted conferences in virtually every Canadian Province and state in the United States.

Besides the books that he has co-authored with Marion, he is the co-author of *Restructuring Schools for Excellence through Teacher Empowerment*, the author of *When the Yellow Jackets Played*, and a companion book, *Yellow Jacket Football in Hard Times and Good*. These books focused on the strengths of the early immigrants who came to America. All of his life Ray has enjoyed sketching, oil painting, and carpentry. The enjoyment of carpentry he considers a gift from his father, father-in-law and grandfathers.

Their email is mjgolarz@live.com

Printed in the United States
By Bookmasters